BEST
DAY EVER

BEST
DAY EVER

D. Adam Goldberg

REGENT PRESS
Berkeley, California

Crafted in the U.S.A.
REGENT PRESS
Berkeley, California
www.regentpress.net

Welcome to BEST DAY EVER

AN INVITATION

SEE WHAT HAPPENS AS WE LOOK AT WORK, FRIENDS,
SPIRITUALITY, SPORTS AND, MOST IMPORTANT,
HAPPINESS, TODAY AND ALWAYS.

YESTERDAY IS GONE
BUT WE LEARN FROM IT.

TOMORROW IS UNCERTAIN
BUT WE PLAN FOR IT.

TODAY, THIS MOMENT, IS WHAT COUNTS.

Contents

CONTENTS

DEDICATION

I would like to dedicate this book
to My Family.

My Mom who has always been there,
every day and moment of my life and
guided me to become the Person I am today.

My Brother and Sister
who have always been there for me.

My Father for always being right?

My Wife Tara and my Daughter Bazil
for their Perfect Love.

All my Friends — for being my Friends.
And for truly knowing me
and loving me anyway.

We are grateful to Mark Weiman,
our Publisher, for working with us
in a sensitive way to create the
special message of
Best Day Ever

Truly,

Adam

1

The Phone Call

Adam, Adam, where are you?

In the Dark

My relationship with my Dad is like a black hole. It's a part of my life that I want to change. I'm going to see Dad. I can make him hear me. I can make him hug me. I know he loves me. I know I love him. Love is powerful. I'm going to tell him how much I love him. I'm going to give him what he wants from me. I still don't know what it is.

I'm hoping to heal our relationship. At least, get along and figure out where to go. I need to be healed. Mom said he told my uncle who told my cousin who told my aunt who told Mom that once he did say he was proud of me. I want to hear ***him say*** he's proud of me. I want to talk about something besides sports, cooking or work. I want him to listen to me, to really hear me. I want him to just once realize that one thing he says is wrong. I want a hug.

I had high hopes.

Adam and Dad

"We're Always Right"!

We're both great arguers. We're both competitive. He's opinion-ated and we're always right! I was telling Dad, "No, that's not right."

He was telling me, "No, *that's* not right. You don't live in the real world."

"You don't live in the real world," I answered. Everybody left the room. "Richard, come back, listen and tell us what you see happening."

Dad said, "No. He'll agree with you."

"Dad, if there were 100 people in here, they'd all agree with me because it is the truth and I am right."

Richard knew better than to get involved. He later told me, "Sometimes it's better to just love somebody instead of fixing them."

"I'm not giving up. I love him too much."

Let's Fix It

Rhonda and I were watching TV. Dad came up and sat right next to me. He was thinking the same thing I was, "Here we go again. Let's fix it."

"Adam, all those things I did that hurt you, I didn't do on pur-pose. I love you and I would never do anything hurtful on purpose. If you told me it was hurtful, I would never do it again."

"Dad, How many times did I ask you not to talk about that subject? Over a hundred times, both at your house and a couple of years ago. Today, I must have asked you not to talk about it 30 or 40 times."

"Well, that's, different. Why do you keep bringing up the past?"

"Dad, you just said you would never do it."

I don't know if he even heard me. He talked over me, rolled his eyes (you know, the **you're an idiot eye roll**), didn't listen, was condescending. He was so rude. I was shaking.

"If I told you you were sitting on the couch, you would have argued that it wasn't a couch."

I looked at Rhonda. "Rhonda, would you help me out here?" Rhonda said nothing.

He stopped. He sighed. "I'm going to bed."

I said, "Give me a kiss, Dad. I love you." I told him I loved him repeatedly.

"Are you saying that if we argue and disagree, you would not love me?"

"No. I just want you to know I love you. I just want to tell you I love you."

He Sighed

He sighed and went to bed. Rhonda said, "Adam, I think he heard you at the end when he sighed." Rhonda and I talked a lot after that. She said, "I don't know why he was arguing. What you said was the truth. I don't think it had anything to do with that."

Bumpy Road Ahead

This was **our way** of connecting. It was his way of provoking me to listen and respond and it was my way of rebelling, proving to myself that he was wrong. The subject of our conversation had nothing to do with what we were talking about! My belief and Dad's belief had nothing to do with the discussion. We just took opposite sides and disagreed. We were mean to each other.

This was a familiar way, maybe the only way we knew. The reason we did it then and the reason we do it now is because it is what

Richard's Taking My Side

we've ***always been doing.*** My Dad hates to do it as much as I do; it's just as hurtful to my Father as it is to me.

The visit was a total failure. Neither reached out. It was painful. It was hard. Richard, Rhonda, Trevor and Taylor felt uncomfortable.

I thought, "Oh no, now I'm messing up their relationship!"

Richard spent more time with our Dad. They've always had a good connection. Now, Richard's taking my side and it might affect his relationship with our Father. The tension was so thick it was hard to breathe.

It's the one relationship, a truly beautiful important relationship that hurts. We need to be healed.

Different Worlds

Writing this book forces growth. He didn't love me in the way I wanted him to love me because his world was different. As I write, I learn, I grow. Tears come.

In my world, we hugged. We kissed. We shared. We danced. We cried. Dad said, "Only sissies cry. Stop crying or I'll give you something to cry about." My Father showed his love in a different way. His way was to buy me clothes, take me to dinner or on a trip. He would give me everything he had if I asked. He would buy us anything. He gave his love to me as things. It was his Father's way. It was not love to me. I need a hug!

Give Me a Break!

I came back from vacation and work in Alaska and Hawaii and hadn't spoken to Dad in over three months. He asked Mom, "Where's Adam? Why won't he return my calls? I don't understand why he is so bitter. I was a good father."

"Adam, Adam, are you there?"

I picked up the phone to call Matt to play volleyball, put the receiver to my ear and heard my Dad say, "Adam, Adam, Adam, are you there?"

I did not want him to be there — but there he was! I had a huge lump in my throat. I wasn't ready. I wanted to talk to him in person.

I Was a Really Good Father

You Needed a Haircut

"Adam, I was a really good father, I don't understand why you are so bitter. Adam, I just don't understand you."

"Father, do you really want to talk about this?

"When I was little and came to see you, you shaved my head."

"I never shaved your head. I got you a haircut. You looked like a hippie. You needed a haircut."

"Dad, it's called a **butch**. It's shaving your head. You threw away my clothes. You tried to get custody of me; you tried to take me away from Mom. You were so harsh. You were strict, so many rules and you made sure I followed them."

"What do you mean, Adam? It was like you were floating in the middle of the ocean on a raft with ragged clothes, no shoes, unkempt hair, eating seaweed and fish. I rescued you from the raft, bought you new shoes and clothes, gave you a bath, fixed your hair and put you on a luxury liner."

"That is a great analogy, Dad, but let me give one to you. I was floating on a raft. I loved to eat fish. We wrapped the fish in seaweed. It's called sushi. I played with the dolphins. I watched the sunset every night. It was my world. It was peaceful. It was what I knew. It was where I was comfortable. You shaved my head, you made me wear shoes, you made me eat with a knife and fork, and you made me drink tea with my pinkie out. When I wanted to watch the sunset, you said it was past my bedtime and told me to go to bed."

"I was a good father. You make me sound like I was bad. You should put some of the good stuff in there. You forgave your Mom. You make her sound like a saint."

Mom

About three nights ago I called my Mom. I can talk to my Mom about anything. No matter what I said, she listened and I would be her Son and she would be my Mom. We cried. We laughed. We shared. We helped each other understand. No judgment, just love.

She loves me and wants to protect me. We talked for a long time about what I should say or do about my Father and me.

"Moma, I can go down there and make my Father think everything is better, pretend to be happy, joke and play as if everything is fine. But, it won't be the truth. It won't be real, neither one of us will be healed. He'll feel better about our relationship. But I won't. There would be no way I could be healed. I've been carrying this around my whole life. It really hurts. I wish I knew how to fix it."

"Stop wanting him to be the Father you never had. Remember all those wonderful men in your life: your brother, coaches, Pop? Just love him as he is."

Back to the Phone Call

"I can talk to Mom, she listens and we work things out."

He said, "What do you mean? We talk."

"Dad, what do we talk about? We talk about sports, work, food; we never talk about anything real."

"What do you mean, **real**?"

"You know, Dad, your health, are you happy? How is your life? What went wrong in our relationship, in my childhood? Do you remember when I came and stayed with you for ten days when I was working in the desert? It was about two years ago. I left without even saying good-bye? Why did I leave? Why was I so hurt? Do you know? You never asked me why I left."

"I think it was something about Shaq."

"That's right, Dad. It was a racist thing that you said about Shaq. I asked you not to talk about it anymore because it bothered me. You would not talk about anything else; you brought it up again and again. I told you repeatedly it was hurtful and you were wrong and I didn't want to talk about it. Why did you keep bringing it up? Why wouldn't you change the subject? Why wouldn't you hear me? You were doing it to hurt me. You identify me with my Mother. When you look at me, you see Mom. I ask you again, why did you keep bringing it up?"

"Adam, I didn't really mean that. That is not what I meant. I don't even believe that."

"If you didn't really mean that and you don't even believe it, then you were doing it to hurt me. And, Dad, you *are* a racist."

"I'm Not a Racist"

"I am not a racist, I have lots of black friends. Hell, I am married to a Mexican."

"Dad, the whole world is racist. I am a racist; you are a racist. You were putting all the different races in categories.

"Dad, you can't tell if somebody is good or bad by the color of their skin or the shape of their eyes. You have to meet them, get to know them to find out if they are good or bad."

He said, "I think that is true. I am not a racist, but that isn't what we were going to talk about, is it?"

"Oh, so now you want to change the subject. Do you really want to talk about it; do you really want to listen? It's hurtful. It's real. It's not the kind of stuff we usually talk about. Okay, Dad, let's talk about it.

I Played Catch With Mom

"Dad, you ask me why I'm so bitter. You're always telling me what a great father you are, right? Are you talking about those games of catch in the front yard? We never played catch. I played catch

You Played Great

with Mom. Sports are a huge part of my life. You did come to a couple of games. You came to that game in Visalia. Do you remember? We were playing College of the Sequoias, the whole Goldberg clan was there."

"Yeah, Adam. It was amazing. You played great. I was proud. I really loved to watch you play."

"That's nice to hear. Do you remember what you said to me after the game?"

"I don't really remember. I do remember being proud and glad that the rest of the family was there to see you play so well."

"Dad, this is what you said, meekly, 'I guess you are a pretty good athlete.'"

"Father, I set the junior college record for all purpose yards in one game. It was the best game I ever played. I played inspired because you were there. I always wanted you to be proud of me."

I Saw Lots of Your Games, Adam

"I saw lots of your games, Adam."

"Lots of my games, Dad? Mom saw every one of my games. She never missed a game. She was the reason I was involved in sports. She took me to youth basketball; when I wanted to quit, she told me, 'You made a commitment.' She went to my practices and my games in Pop Warner Football. In Pony League, our coach had a heart attack after the first practice. They got all the parents together and said, 'We need someone to help.' Nobody stepped forward except Mom.

"Guess who hit infield practice? She never missed a game. When I was at San Jose State, she drove to all of my games: Arizona, Utah in her VW Bug.

"Dad, you saw three of my games: two junior college football games and one junior college basketball game against Cuesta College. It was the best game I played at Cabrillo. I was inspired: I wanted you to be proud of me. You never told me you were proud of me."

"What do you mean? I am so proud of you. I am proud. I'm proud. I'm proud, proud, proud, proud, proud."

"Dad, that doesn't mean anything. That is not from your heart. You are just saying that because I said you've never said it."

"Adam, I really am proud of you."

"Thank you, Dad; that is really nice to hear."

"Adam, I loved to watch you play. I wish I could have seen every game. I was working. I lived in Mexico."

"You went to Tucson every other weekend; you went to Bakersfield once a month. *If it had been important to you, you would have been there.*"

"I had a job. I had to work. I was working."

"Dad, we're not getting anywhere. You're not hearing me."

"Adam, you're not hearing me. I was a good father. You're so bitter. I am not a racist. You are not letting me talk."

Adam, Tudah and the VW

"You Made Up a Lie"

"Father, our relationship sucks. Remember when we were kids, we went to Tucson. Grandma and Grandpa Goldberg lived there. About every other time, you'd say we had to visit Grandma and Grandpa. You never wanted to go. You'd make up a lie and told it to us; in case they asked why we had to leave so soon, we'd all have the same story. You know, we have to leave in 15 minutes. You told me you didn't want us to have the same relationship you had with your Father. Guess what, Dad? We do. Do you want to work on our relationship? Or, do you want to keep the one we got?"

"Adam, you don't have a choice whether or not to have a relationship with me. I'm your Father."

"I'm your Son and you're my Father. I'm asking you if you want to keep the relationship we have or make it better. We could be the best Father and Son duo ever!

"Are you there? Father, are you hearing me? What do you want to do about our relationship? Dad, are you listening?"

"Adam, you're not hearing me. I was a good father."

2

Coming to Light

Forgive but don't blame me

dam, you said we are so much alike. If we are so much alike, you must be a really bad person."

We Don't Listen

"You're right, Dad, we are so much alike. The ways that we are alike are beautiful, not bad. I am trying to be a better listener. I find myself doing exactly what you are doing."

"What do you mean? I'm a good listener, what am I doing?"

"It's the same thing I do. When someone talks, we don't listen. We are thinking, 'They are wrong. I know the answer to this question.' Or, if we think they are right, we are thinking, 'I can say that better.' We don't really hear their thought; we just hear pieces. Instead of listening, we are formulating our response, which we are sure is right. Because, we both know we are always right."

While We Were Talking

It happened while we were talking. I can't explain it — how it happened or what caused it. In an instant, my total attitude altered. A whole different world grabbed my thoughts. I changed and the change was amazing. I didn't *feel* different, I was still me. I was standing in a new spot, looking at Dad in a bright, unusual way. It was as if a floodlight flared on another half or part of my Father that before was a dark shadow. Now, I was seeing him as a whole person. I saw that the things he was trying to instill in me were good, caring qualities that I didn't have and that I needed.

Do You Like Ginger?

"When I was a kid, there was one thing we always enjoyed doing together. We were connected, Father and Son. I had you all to myself. Richard never liked to do it. Do you remember what it was?"

Coming to Light

"I don't know. Why don't you tell me?"

"Cooking, remember? You'd come and say, 'Adam, do you want to cook? I am going to make something. How about Chinese? I love our Chinese? Do you like ginger? How about ginger beef?'"

"I'd get my stool and come stand on it close to you in the kitchen. You told me all the things we needed to get and we would get them together. You were passionate about our cooking. You loved it and I loved it.

"I am still passionate about cooking. You were a great teacher. You'd tell me, 'Cut the ginger a little bit finer. It's too strong a spice to use that big.' You'd have me taste all of the spices. We prepared it together. 'Not too much garlic. If you use too much, it takes over and that is all you can taste.'"

"You don't like garlic?" And you said, "I like it but people use it too much and then it is all that you can taste in the cooking."

"I tell my friends that when I cook."

"I remember it all, Adam. I loved to cook with you and loved that you loved it too. You really listened to me."

"Father, I don't think you are a bad person. If I could pick any other father in the world, I would pick you every time. I got so much good stuff from you."

"I think so."

"Dad, not just cooking but the way you love to entertain. You can make friends with anybody, the president or the janitor. You were nice to everybody regardless of their status in life.

"Your smile. I have the same smile, you know, those smiling, squinty eyes. Your mannerisms, the way you hold yourself, the way you talk with your hands. You are a great leader. You're the boss at the ranch. Everybody loves you.

"We ate with the people that worked for you, not as your boss but as one of them. They accepted you. You treated all of them the same."

The Same Smile

The Same Smile

Mom Never Said No

"Mom really never said **No**; you said **No** a lot. You were giving me direction, responsibility, discipline and order. You made me bathe twice a day; when I got out of the shower, you would inspect me and tell me I didn't use any soap. You scrubbed my fingernails. The truth is I would just get wet. It was the right thing to do. I am sorry.

"Father, are you there? Are you hearing me?"

"Well, what is wrong with that? I was trying to instill in you some of my ways of life and give you direction where you had none."

There was a long pause.

Then, I poured my heart out to him. I realized that he was helping — he was fathering me. "Dad, I realize you were being a father, you were trying to help and protect me, to help me be a better person. The problem was, I was a rebellious little hippie."

"Adam, I worried about you. You never had any money."

Life Was Easy

"I was comfortable with my world. I was street smart. I could take care of myself. Mom liked to play bridge. We used to go to a place in Santa Cruz called *The Catalyst.* It was downtown on the

Mall. I was 10. Kelly and I went out on the Mall and told people we were stranded and needed money for the bus to get home. In 15 minutes, we had $30.00, enough for the movies, ice cream and popcorn. Other times, we went to the beach and the boardwalk. Life was easy. It was free, no rules, no boundaries, just play.

The Exact Thing I Needed

"It was a world I was good at. Your world of structure, rules and order was a world I was not comfortable with. I had to be accountable. Instead of seeing it as the exact thing I needed — you doing your job being my father — seeing my weaknesses and teaching me what I needed to know to be a complete person, I rebelled against your authority. I lied and told you what you wanted to hear. I thought you were mean. I didn't understand you. You treated me different than you treated Richard, because you saw so much of my Mother in me and because I took her side."

My Father wasn't hearing me and I had no idea where I was going.

Missing My Father

"Dad, that was my world, I was a hippie. I thought you were wrong. You tried to put me in your world and I was not comfortable there.

"Father, thank you for caring about me. The things you did needed to be done. I needed direction. I didn't see it as love, but it was love. If it weren't for you, I wouldn't have the work ethic I have. I wouldn't have table manners. The problem was I was a hippie eleven months of the year. I was from a different world. I was with you for one month a year and you gave me a year's worth of fathering in that one month.

"Instead of learning, instead of seeing you as helping me, loving me, giving me manners and structure, I saw it as punishment. Thank you, Father. It was the right thing to do. It's just now that I'm grasping it. The fatherly things that you did for me were just what I was missing in my life. I was missing my Father.

Don't Blame Me

"I apologize to you from the bottom of my heart. *Please forgive me, but don't blame me.* I was living in a different world; I thought your world was wrong. Your world was right, my world was right; the problem was I was only in your world for one month a year. You fought for us, you called us twice a week, you tried to get custody of us because you loved us. You wanted me to be more like you, to have more of your qualities. You were right. I needed more direction. I needed to know that following the rules is a good thing. I love you for caring and trying so hard to help me. You have always been a great provider and role model. I am sorry I was so rebellious."

Dad, Are You Listening?

"Dad, are you there? Are you listening? Hello Father, are you there????!!!!!!"

"I am not a racist."

"Dad did you hear what I said, did you hear anything I said? Pull over, close your eyes and listen. This is the most important thing I have ever said to you. Please hear me."

I repeated it all. I said it with love in my heart. I said it with passion.

"Dad, can you respond to that?"

He said "Well, what do you want me to say, Adam. I was too harsh. I love you, what do you want me to say?"

"Dad, I want you to respond. I want you to hear me. This is the most meaningful conversation we have ever had. I am telling you what a great Father you were and are and I am sorry and you are not hearing me."

"Well, I am not from your world. I can't respond in a way that is acceptable for you."

Dad started arguing his point, telling me he was right.

"I am not from your world, I can't respond in a way that you will accept."

"Dad, take the same scenario, let's say that it is two idiots or two geniuses, a father and son, people we don't even know. Their relationship is not what it could be; in fact, it is bad. Are you listening?"

"Yes."

"Please, this is so important to me. I want you to hear me and respond; I want to hear what you have to say. These two people are talking. The son pours his heart out to the father. *I repeated the story above.* And his father's response was, 'I am not a racist.'"

You Taught Me Something Today

With compassion and love, he said, "That is terrible. I am sorry I didn't hear you. Adam, I love you. I am so proud of you. I am sorry for teasing you. You taught me something today. Thank you. I love you and I am sorry for all the hurtful things.

"I want to work on our relationship. I love you with all my heart and you are a great son.

"If you wanted me to go to Alaska and wait there for you in the freezing cold, I'd go and wait until you came or I froze to death."

"Dad, when I look in the mirror, I see you."

My father heard me for the first time in my life.

We're on our way.

3

On Our Way

It wasn't all your fault!

My Father heard me for the first time in my life. I have talked to him every day since. Right now, he is in intensive care in Eisenhower Medical Center. Richard, my dog Moses and I are on our way to see Dad. We are thinking and

On Our Way to See Dad

talking a lot about our relationship with our Father — the things we did when we were kids. I was seeing my Father in a new light.

He called us twice a week our whole lives. He put my brother through college in style. He bought us both new cars when we graduated from high school. Whenever we saw him, we would always do things together. We went fishing. He took us to the best lakes in Mexico. He was a great fisherman. When we went fishing, he showed us how and then enjoyed watching us. He got more out of seeing us catch one fish then if he had caught fifty. He is the best cook in the world. His lunches were unbelievable.

We Went Fishing

An Amazing Man, My Dad

I said that my Father showed love by buying things for us and that that was the way his Father showed love to him. But that is not the whole truth. That is what I *chose* to dwell on. The truth is, he is an amazing man. As long as I can remember, he has gotten up at 4:00 in the morning, showers, dresses and has some juice. Then, comes into our room, "Come on. Let's go to the ranch. I'm going to barbecue for everybody. Adriana's making tortillas and salsa and I'm bringing the rest. Get up. Let's go to the ranch."

A Hard Worker

He has always been such a hard worker. He works so hard because he loves to take care of his family. He loves to buy us things. I cannot remember him buying much for himself. He is a giver. He loves me. He really is proud of me. I couldn't be more proud of him. My Father has been a rich man and he has been a poor man. When he was rich, he shared it with the world; and, when he was poor, he shared what he had with the world.

Dad Lit Up Like a Christmas Tree

We drove straight to the hospital. When we got there, he was in Radiology. They told us to come back in twenty minutes. We walked into the room to push the button to get in to see him. We never got to the button. Right then, someone came over the intercom, "Is there somebody out there waiting to see Frederick Goldberg?" The girl sounded agitated; she had made the mistake of telling him that Richard and Adam were there to see him.

As we entered, we saw the nurse getting him off the gurney. I told Richard we'd better wait, "If he sees us, he'll get too excited and tear something." We walked into the room. We were both excited. Dad lit up like a Christmas tree. He smiled like a mouse eating cheese. When I looked at him, it was like looking in the mirror. I saw my smile. I saw my eyes — those squinty, smiling eyes looking back at me.

When I Look in the Mirror, I See Dad

Nothing But Good

We were seeing nothing but the good. We laughed. We told jokes. We flirted with nurses. John, a friend of his came by. Dad was so gracious. He told John what a great friend he had been to him. He introduced us, "This is my son Adam."

"Oh, the one that runs the motorhome dealership? Your dad is always bragging about you. You're the athlete right? He told me about the game he went to. He said his whole family was there. He is so proud of you."

"This is my other son Richard."

"Oh, you run the computers for all of Texaco? Your dad told me about your sons and your wife. He said he is really proud of your relationship."

"Nice to meet you John. How do you know Dad?"

"He is one of my best friends."

Somebody named Anthony calls him on his cell phone.

Dad says, "Anthony? Let me talk to him. Hi Anthony. It's Papa Fred." Dad talks to him in Spanish. Everybody loves my Dad. So much so that later that day they moved him out of his room into a suite because he had too many visitors.

John tells us he is in the compost business.

I said, "Dad, didn't you mention something about a guy who cooked a turkey in a pile of compost?" We all laugh. John says, "I am the guy."

I'm amazed. "I thought Dad was putting me on."

John says, "No. I have this big thermometer, about five feet long. I go around and find a hot spot. It has to be over 175 degrees. I try to find the hottest spot. I put the turkey into two oven bags and bury it for 24 hours. Your dad says it's the best turkey he ever ate."

Dad's a good cook. I am thinking that he is lying. We laugh. We tell jokes. Right then, Adriana calls. I answer the phone, "IRS" dead silence. "Adriana, is that you."

"You scared me. Can I talk to your father?"

"We're busy. He's got 15 guests here."

" Yeah, I bet 12 of them are nurses."

I tell everybody what she said. We all laugh hysterically. We had some serious talk. We told him how much we loved him and he told us how much he loved us. He told us what great sons we were. I apologized to him for blaming him for not seeing his love for what it really was. I thanked him for being a great Father.

He said, "It wasn't all your fault."

It Wasn't Long Enough

We stayed for about three hours. It wasn't long enough. Dad was falling asleep; "I'm not sleepy, Son, I'm just resting my eyes". Dad needed to sleep. Rich and I kiss and hug him and he tells us how much he loves us. I am feeling it in every part of my heart and soul.

We Paced the Floor

We both had so much fun with Dad that we didn't want to leave. It was the best conversation and the most loving and caring time I have ever spent with my Father in my life. Richard said to me, "It was the nicest time I have ever spent with him." It was so fun being with him; we were feeling his love for us.

He was so affectionate. He was holding our hands. It seemed so perfect.

It seemed so easy. It seemed so simple. That night, *Richard and I paced the floor, trying to mull over what happened, how this change came about.*

"Just Resting My Eyes"

I can't wait to see Dad tomorrow. It's going to be really hard to have a better day than today, but I am positive it is going to be better. It is so simple to dwell on the good. It feels so much better to see the beauty, to see the caring, to see the love. It's 1:30 in the morning. I keep asking Richard if he is tired. He says, "No. I am just resting my eyes!!!!"

Rich, Moses and I are driving to see Dad. It's a beautiful day. We've got the top down, best parking place in the hospital, the only one with shade for Moe. I can't wait to see Dad.

My Best Day Ever

Dad's lying in his bed in Eisenhower Hospital, recovering from open heart surgery. He looks at us with tears in his eyes. I have never seen him cry.

"How do you feel, Dad, how are you feeling right now? I have never felt so close to you."

And Dad says, "Son, this is my Best Day Ever. If they cut my heart out today, it would still be my *Best Day Ever.*"

4

Adam, This Book is for You

As I write it, it writes me

The amazing Light that changed my attitude toward my Father inspired me to write this book. I quit a great job to write *Best Day Ever.* I've learned much writing it; as I write it, it writes me. My Pop said, "Adam, this book is for you." Yes, it is for me and I hope for you. I am still learning. This is what I was shown.

Adam, This Book is for You

A Perfect Story That Hasn't Been Written

At the moment the child is conceived, the child is without flaw. She is perfect. He is perfect. No bad habits. Pure love, pure joy, totally honest, unafraid. Never been lied to and never lied. *A spotless slate — a perfect story that hasn't been written.*

Smart, Like Me!

Their learning experiences come from their parents and their environment. Their learning and teaching and their nourishment to live and grow as human beings come from us. We are their environment. Our children absorb us, not the persons we pretend to be, but who we really are. They speak the same language. They walk like us.

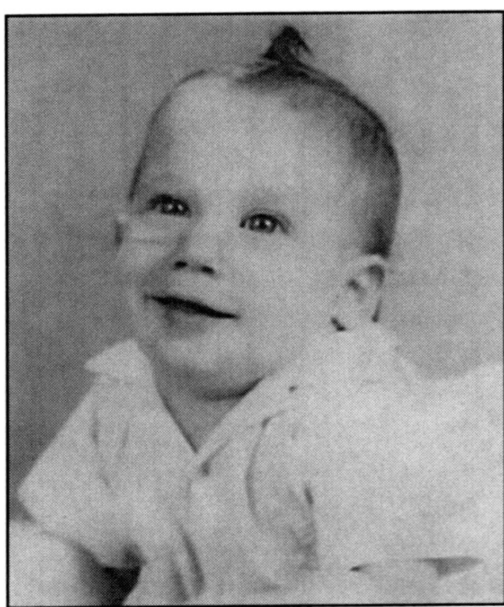

A Spotless Slate

They have the same smiles, the same frowns. They are interested in the same subjects. Think about the families you know: the parents and the children are similar. They speak English. They speak Spanish. They speak French. They don't just speak the same language, they have the same accents! The children are a product of their role models and their environment.

Parents Write the Story

If your parents are farmers, you might not be a farmer, but you'd know a lot about farming. If you're raised in a constant state of war, you'd be a warrior — you'd fight for a cause that someone else believed in and you'd fight even if you don't believe in it. You probably wouldn't have a choice. TV shows us children: 11, 12, 13 years old, fighting wars, carrying guns, killing for a cause they know little about. A story they were told by their parents. Do they want to fight those wars? Some of them would, because it's what they know. *When they were born, their slate was clear; this was how their slate was filled. This is the story their parents wrote for them.*

Tiger Woods

Not just their parents, but also the environment they were born into. Maybe it's right for them to fight; the war might be just. Take that same child the day he was born; give him to Tiger Woods' parents. Would he be a warrior? Or, one of the world's greatest golfers?

Think about our responsibility to write on that empty slate. It's the single most important privilege and purpose we will ever be blessed with; and the hardest and the greatest honor we will ever know.

Born Holy?

We start as a perfect being. For most of our lives, we strive to be perfect, to be holy, honest, open. Guess what? *We were perfect. What happened?*

We make mistakes. We lie. We cheat. We do things we know are wrong. There is no good without bad. If we had a perfect upbringing, parents who were perfect role models; if we were never lied to; whenever we spoke, we were heard; when we were spoken to, we listened and did what we were told, would we be perfect?

Born Rebellious

Would we have world peace? Would the world be perfect without war, starvation, greed, racism, crime? No. It *would* be a better world. *Rebellion is stamped into our human nature;* if we're raised as vegetarians, we want a burger. The Amish children are nurtured in a very special environment. A small percentage might stay on the farm, choose to live the way they were raised by their parents. The rest? They want to go to the city; they want to drive fast cars. They want to be rock stars!

They Follow My Lead

When I see the truth in these words, I know I'm going to be a better parent. I won't be able to compose a perfect slate. No one can be a perfect parent. But, if I am good and loving, there's a good chance they'll be good and loving. If I listen to them when they talk, they'll be better listeners; if I run and play with them, they'll

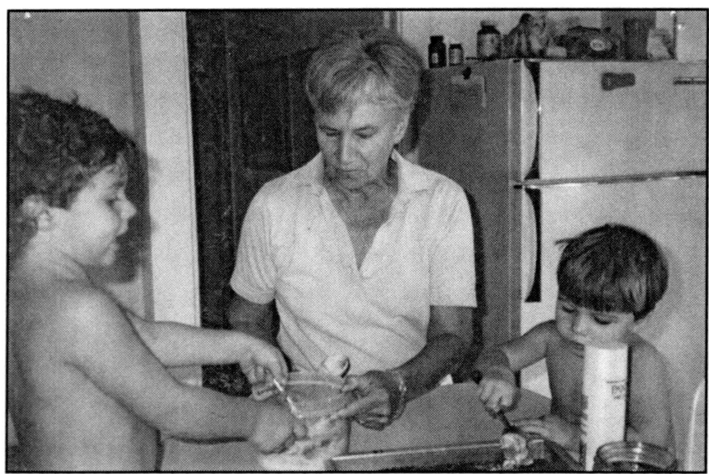

Writing on the Slate

run and play. If I hug and kiss them, they'll be better huggers and kissers. If I'm a good role model, they will tend to follow my lead.

Be the Person You Want Your Child to Be

Take this into your heart. Take this into your soul. When we hear the truth, we know the truth. They start perfect. They are a reflection of us. When you look at your reflection, what do you see? Do you like what you see? Can you do better? Can you be a better person? Can you be more loving? Yes. Of course you can.

If you're going to have children or if you have children, do the right thing. You know the difference between wrong and right. Write your best picture on that slate. *Be the person you want your child to be.* It will help you. It will help them.

5

Adam's Slate

I kept my thoughts like a secret

A dam was born to Marjorie Joan (Johana) Moon and Frederick Wells Goldberg in Bakersfield, California on July 30, 1961 at 9:15 in the morning. Adam has a brother Richard, who is a year and four months older. His sister Jerilee is 10 years older.

By Mom

Adam beamed into the world with a rush, as though he couldn't wait to be with us. (Later, he told us, "When I get born again, I want to be in the same family.") He was a joyful, happy baby, darling with blond curls. He glowed. I adored him. Adam didn't talk much; he was a quiet, happy watcher of life. He cherished his brother Richard. Richard talked for him. Adam and Richard were and are very close. Richard was Best Man at Adam and Tara's wedding.

I Remember Dorothy

When I was old enough to crawl, we crawled to Santa Cruz. I had a very loving, open childhood. We had horses, a cat and a pet duck named **Dorothy.** Mom wanted to get back to nature. She was

Joyful, Happy Child

a free spirit, searching for something, an adventuress. We lived in the back of a horse pasture in a 21 foot trailer, which Mom bought for a couple hundred bucks. We painted it brown and thought it was "ducky". Dorothy slept with us and quacked whenever anyone came to see us. She was our watch duck. Dorothy kept guard and followed us wherever we went.

Our horses were right outside our front door. I loved the trailer and the horse pasture. The Bird Sanctuary — a 100-acre natural reserve on the edge of a lagoon — was our playground, a wilderness

Ollaberries Everywhere!

with ollaberries everywhere. It was a great place to live and grow. It was beautiful. It was all nature and natural, a wonderful place for a kid to grow and learn.

Remember Dorothy, Moma? Remember the tree house — the one you said was way too high?

Dorothy, Our Watch Duck

Mom Was Searching

Mom was searching. I searched with her. We searched together. We went Sufi dancing, slept on the beach, rode our ponies, picked berries and ate food from our garden. We did everything together. My Mom was my best friend, my soul mate and partner. We were bonded. My life was utter bliss. She smiled. She loved me. My Mother was a great mother, loving, always loving and caring. When I tell her how much I love her, the only way I can tell her how much I love her is to tell her I love you just as much as you love me. We smiled. We played. We raised our horses. We grew together.

Richard moved to live with Dad in Mexico. He didn't like the trailer. I missed him.

The Gangster

One of her boyfriends was a gangster, a drug dealer. Mom says she didn't know he was a drug dealer. I did. I was nine. I love the gangster still. He still loves me. We moved a lot. We moved to a house in the country — a beautiful house. We rented our rooms. I have great memories of that house and the people we lived with. I still think about Angelina. She was a dancer and an actress. She used to stretch out a lot — naked in the sun!

Not Good at "No"

Mom wasn't good at "No"; I'm not either. There wasn't a whole lot of structure, but oh so much love, so much understanding, so much compassion. Mom was all about love. She was about understanding. She was happy. She was fun. She loved me. She loved everybody. She was a free spirit.

She always wanted to fix things *now*. If we had a fight, she wanted to fix it. She didn't want to pretend like it wasn't there. She wanted to find the problem and fix it now! Now, right *now*.

We Road Our Ponies

Pillow Talk

When we had problems or fights, we'd have problem solving meetings. Mom wrote down our ideas to solve the problem. We could take any solution off the list until we got down to a couple, until we had a few left that would work for everybody. When I had problems or fights, she would have me do Gestalt. I'd take a pillow that represented the other person. I told them (the pillow) how I felt and what was bothering me. Then, I switched to be on the pillow and be the other person and talk back.

Teacher Mom

Mom was special. She taught parenting. She taught parents how to be better parents, mostly through active listening. She taught people to listen and hear. She was a counselor and specialized in Gestalt Therapy. She trained foster parents for Santa Cruz County. Whenever she discovered something she thought was helpful, she'd bring it home and teach it to us.

Free School

When I first started school, I went to my Mom's school. It was part of the Santa Cruz Community School. We called it a *free school*, free, because the curriculum was developed around the children, not the children stuck into the curriculum. We learned to dance, sew, draw, and cook. We played, talked and sang. One of our favorite songs was *Yesterday*. We sang it over and over.

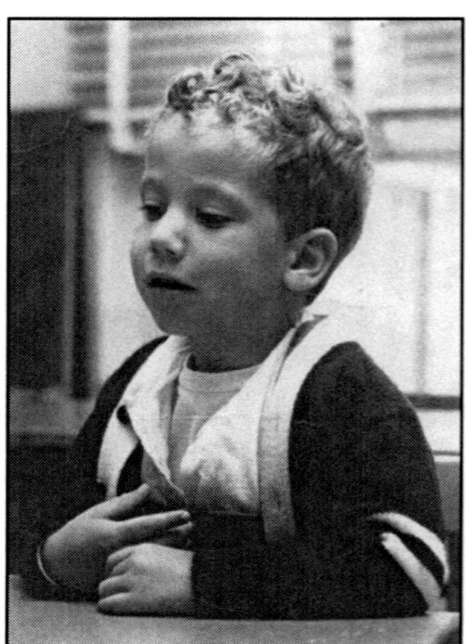

Think For Ourselves

Outside the Box

Mom started the free school because of us. She wanted us to learn, not just reading and writing, she

Parent Training Topic

Family Service Association of orthern Santa Cruz County ill present another in its series workshop programs Monday 8 p.m. at Holiday Inn.

Speaker will be Johana Goldrg, who will discuss "Parent aining — Another Way of eing With Your Child." lmission is $2.50 per person free to all members of the mily Service association.

Mrs. Goldberg, instructor at brillo College, is a former sociate and a friend of Dr. avid E. Smith who was iginally scheduled to speak at e workshop. Dr. Smith, founr and medical director of the ight-Ashbury Free Medical inic, is unable to keep the eaking engagement Monday ening but will be scheduled at ater date, it was announced.

Mrs. Goldberg has taught any groups of parents how to 1ear" their children more fectively and accurately, and w to communicate in ways at the children can underand more clearly. She helps rents to free themselves of eviously learned non-working ethods of relating to their ildren, and provides practical d simple guidelines that are offshoot of Thomas Gordon's cently popularized book, ARENT EFFECTIVENESS RAINING.

including a master's degree from University of San Francisco. However, she feels her most relevant training came from a self-designed curriculum which includes participation in the Gestalt Training Institute in San Francisco, working in Gestalt with the late Fritz Perls at Esalon, with Effectiveness Training Associates in San Francisco and Bakersfield, and as an associate with Dr. Richard Suchman at the Ortega Park Teacher Training Laboratory.

As well as a teacher, Mrs. Goldberg is a mother, a grandmother (hard to believe when one sees her) and a warm and personable woman. M.K.

JOHANA GOLDBERG

wanted us to grow, to create our own paths. *Mom wanted us to think for ourselves and have an education that connected learning with our minds and our hearts.* She wanted us to know it was okay to take our own path. We were living outside of the box.

Spell "Phone" For Me

Mom designed an easy spelling system, combining shorthand symbols and phonics. If a vowel sounded like an "A" instead of "ah", we put two dots over the vowel. Spell "knew". We spelled it *NU.* We put two dots over the *U.* This changes the sound to be *U* Instead of *UH*, such as *under.* This is one example of what we did in our school. A nu concept: "Anser the fon, ples." Get it? It was so simple. It was so simple that our school of eight children wrote, published and sold our own book (it sold out!) — everyone free to express and write their own way. It's the way it should be. Spell "phone" for me. The problem was, everybody outside of the school, knew the world was flat! We were the only ones using our spelling system!

EST

When I was about 12, I went to EST. Mom said I had to go. Richard and Jerilee went also. Werner Erhardt did my training. EST — did you get it? I got it. Well, what is it? You said you got it. I did get it. I'm still not sure what it is. No one would ever tell you what you were supposed to have got. But I think I got it. ??????

Public School

When I went to public school, the fourth grade teacher, suspicious of my spelling skills, wanted me to be tested. The test showed that I was above average in most subjects. My test went off the chart with the highest score ever achieved in the topic of *putting ideas together.*

If I had a subject or a teacher that I liked, I got *A's.* In the second grade, my teacher Miss Pini created a special award for me, which she said was for my kindness to every person in the class.

They Knew I Was Wrong or Tha Nu I Waz Rong

I still can't spell; I never learned to write in cursive. They thought I was retarded because I spelled different. I asked questions. I disagreed. They knew I was wrong before they heard the question. The truth is they weren't interested in my question and they didn't even hear it.

I had a great education. I had four years of college. Even though I wasn't book trained, I did better than get by. I made friends with my teachers and got good enough grades to play sports. I had a great education, education of life. I listened, learned, watched and saw everything. I took it all in. I learned and learned and learned. I grew as a person, every minute every day.

Regrets

Mom reminisces about our wild life and wonders if she should have rather created a solid home life for us. You know, a stable environment, mom, dad and white picket fence — a nurturing, steady home for the whole family.

"If I could change the past, I would do it different, better."

Can We Move Back?

"Mom, you were searching, changing and growing. You were growing and I was growing with you. If we weren't searching, if we weren't growing, we would never have taken this path. We wouldn't know all the wonderful things we now share. What about the beach? We barbecued every night; we played on the beach. We swam. We watched the sunset. Can we move back?

I Kept Them Like a Secret

"Mom, I wouldn't change a thing. The story you wrote was perfect. You wrote it just for me. I could dance. I could paint. I could sing. I could knit. I could listen. I loved people. I thought for myself. *Even if they told me my thoughts were wrong, I kept them like a secret. I still believe.*

If Things Were Different, I wouldn't be Me —
When the Higher Spirit created mothers, he created a perfect one for me. *Mom, if things were different, I wouldn't be me and, think about it — would you be you?"*

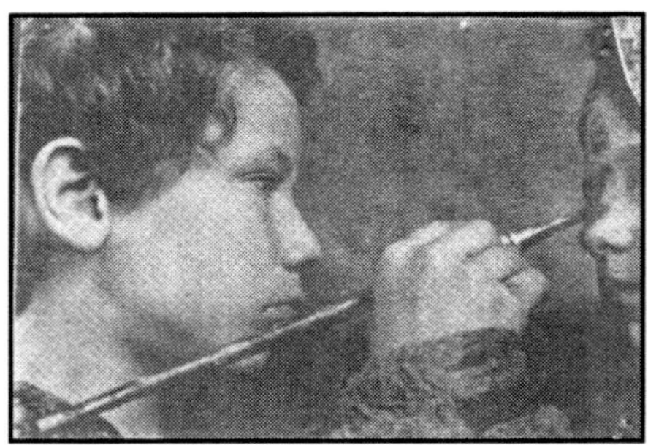

I Could Paint — I Could Dance

6

Hey, Sport!

It's the flow!

But, what I really liked was Sports!
Sports have been a huge part of my life.

At Balboa

I Love Sports

I made it through school mostly because of sports. I was blessed with mad skills. I was MVP in peewee basketball: MVP of the team, MVP in the league. When I was in eighth grade, I went to Santa Cruz County Olympics and was outstanding athlete. And it continued like that through college.

What a Wonderful World!

I got a lot out of sports: acknowledgment, popularity, and the development of leadership qualities. I was passed through high school because of my sports ability. I went to junior college, played basketball and football and was MVP of the team and of the Coast Conference. I led the Coast Conference in *all purpose yards,* and got a scholarship to San Jose State to play football. I had no transferable

**Receiving Golden Helmet MVP Award From
Coach Joe Marvin of Cabrillo College**

units, no high school degree. What a wonderful world!

I broke OJ Simpson's record for all purpose yards in a single game. My Father was there with the whole Goldberg family. It was one of the few games that he saw me play and it was my best game ever.

What is a Sport?

What is a sport? It's whatever we do when we compete, when we want to win. Sports is an agreement to fight a war to the very best of our efforts according to rules all parties agree to follow.

If you just knew me from the field or court, you wouldn't think I was a very nice person. Everybody I played with said I was/am two different people. I'm a really nice guy off the court and I'm tenacious, ruthless, on the court. I have a great desire to win.

They're wrong. I'm the same guy. It's part of my game. I don't like to lose. I like to win. In sports, we all know people who say, "We played our best and we lost. Our effort was sincere. We couldn't have played better." Loser! *The team that wants to win the most — deep in their hearts — is the team that wins.*

What's Trash Talk?

Do you talk trash when you play sports? What is talking trash? It's part of competitive sports. It's when you say or do anything to take someone out of their game, show them you're superior, get in their head, get their focus off of winning.

Get the Ball and Run

When I was eight, Mom signed me up for basketball. The first game, I was so excited that every time I got the ball, I didn't dribble, I grabbed it, held on tight and ran. Mom said, "You weren't the worst. One of the kids sat on the ball." That's right, he just took the ball and sat on it.

By the third or fourth game, I caught on and played basketball all day, every day. By the end of that season, I was the best player in the league. Mom went to all my games.

"Everybody — Let's Play!"

Sports molded a lot of my qualities. It taught me to be a leader, a very vocal point guard. "Come on. Let's play now — defense — everybody — let's play!" And the whole tempo of the game changed.

My Coach Made the Difference

What a difference a good coach makes! And what a difference faith makes! Have you ever had a coach that had so much faith in you that you couldn't let him down? You *couldn't* fail? You'd do anything for him? My coach had so much faith in me. He knew about the sports flow. When I say "flow", I mean the way things work, the cohesion. It's the way things work when you're playing perfect. It's effortless. It just flows.

"I'm the Greatest!"

Sometimes I sound so conceited. When I read this book, it sounds like I think I'm a saint. I apologize. If and when we meet, I'm sure it's not the way you'll feel. Remember Dion Sanders, Prime Time? I always told people I loved Dion. They didn't like how arrogant he was — just the best football player ever. I always said he came from a different part of town. It was cool in his part of town to act the way he acted, dress the way he dressed — gold chains and all. They said he was conceited. I don't think it's conceited to say you're the best when you believe it's the truth. For him, I think it was.

Coach Enzweiler

A coach I want to mention is Bob Enzweiler. I loved to be with Coach Enzweiler. He had tremendous faith in me and I had tremendous faith in him. We worked together. We coached as one: I coached on the floor and he coached on the sidelines. I was an extension of him. We both made mistakes but we were a great team.

Coach Enzweiler died of brain cancer about five years ago. I miss him. But, he's alive inside me. He gave me a lot and I cherish him. This is a letter Coach wrote to my mother:

HARBOR BASKETBALL
300 LA FONDA AVENUE, SANTA CRUZ, CA 95065
BOB ENZWEILER, COACH

May 15, 1969

Johana,

Just a note to tell you how much I enjoy Adam! I know you appreciate the confidence I have in Adam but you may not know how I appreciate his confidence in me. I never had a player with so much insight into personal feelings.

Friday night I had to reprimand the team for their attitude; as Adam left, he just put his arm around me letting me know what I did was right.

One of the best rewards in coaching is your relationship with your players and Adam and mine is one I will not forget. Richard is a great kid too. It has not been easy for you without a husband but what a super job!

Love,

Bob

GO

Sports are my therapy. The sports high is one of the very best. When I get a ball, I go out on the court or the field, and nothing **else** is there. I don't think about anything else. It's the only thing. I don't think about anything except the sport, the victory and how to beat them. *Think* is not the right term. I react. What makes it therapy for me is that I don't think. I react. I flow. I'm in my element — nothing there but the ball, the other team and GO.

Next Time

It isn't always fun — not always good. I missed the shot that would have won the game. It's my fault. I played terrible. I was open but nobody would throw me the ball. I was injured. It was his fault. Our coach made too many mistakes. He yelled at me. He took me out of the game when we were ahead and the team needed me.

Next time I'm going to make that shot. I'm going to play better. He's going to coach better, have a better scheme. I talked to him and he's not going to yell at me anymore. Sports are like life — lifelike! God! I Love sports.

Learn From the Bad

What's he talking about? Does this sound like gibberish? Is that what you're thinking? I'm talking about life. I'm talking about learning. Learning from the bad things, realizing that, in life and in sports and everything that we do, there's no good without bad. There's no bad without good. Learn from the bad. Turn it into good. This is the place. Work on your shot. Talk to your coach. Do better. I love sports. I love life. See the good. Learn from the bad. Win. Win. Win. Win. Just win, baby. Go Raiders. Love the Raiders.

BUD LIGHT BUD LIGHT BUD LIGHT

7

Follow the Leader

Milk and cookies

Follow Me

I had a coach Jerry McGowen. He changed my life. He was the seventh and eighth grade coach at Aptos. He had coached big time college basketball. I'm not sure where he coached before or why he was now coaching at a little school in Santa Cruz County. He was one of those coaches who had great faith in me and encouraged leadership abilities. We never lost a game in two years. We flowed. We were one. We worked together. I was MVP both years.

Because of Coach, we developed tenacity, heart and played to the top of our ability. We played better than the top of our ability. We all played our best. We went more than one hundred percent all of the time. It was a joy. It was stepping outside myself. I gave it everything I had but I got so much more out of it.

He was positive. He was always positive. *He found something good in anything bad you ever did.* He was a true leader, a true leader.

Are These Leaders?

Are these leaders: a president, a general, a team captain? Maybe.

A leader is that person who inspires, elevates, encourages and touches the lives of others. Not because they are appointed, elected or designated as the leader but because they live life in such a way that others want to follow them.

A leader is somebody who is honest, somebody who knows the answers. Someone who can share the answers with you, someone who's secure. Leaders are friendly. They are not arrogant. They are friendly with everybody. They're friendly with the President; they're friendly with the Refuse Disposal Technician. They can apologize. They realize that their followers or the people they are leading probably know as much as they about whatever endeavor they are leading. There can be leadership moments too, moments in time when others are inspired to lead and you are inspired to follow. Are you a follower? Are you a leader? Do you aspire to be a leader?

An Innate Ability

Leaders welcome the experiences and expertise of others. They learn. They are great listeners. When they speak, people listen. They take charge of situations, but not necessarily control. They don't kill the messenger. They don't look for someone to blame. They are part of the solution and part of the problem. The leader is willing to say, "I was wrong. I made a mistake. I take responsibility for it." And they learn from it. *The leader has an innate ability to see what needs to be done and a spiritual quality that rouses others to see what they see and want to go with their vision.*

A Gift and a Curse

The leader naturally inspires confidence in others. It's not something they do on purpose or try to do. It's natural. It's a gift and a curse. It's a curse because it carries a demanding responsibility. What's hard about it? Sometimes the leader leads down the wrong path. A true leader believes it is the right way to go. They feel responsible. They are responsible. At the same time, they will admit they were wrong and correct it. It is still a tough responsibility.

The Leader Follow*s*

Can a leader also be a follower? Without a shadow of a doubt, true leaders know when to follow. It is not so important if you lead or follow. ***It's walking your path that matters most.***

I live in the United States. I follow most of the rules. I follow the Government's decisions. I don't speed. I don't cross the double yellow line. I stop at the stop signs. I even pay my taxes; well, I've paid a lot of taxes. Following the lead of our Government is usually the right thing to do. I don't like all of their decisions. I don't like all of their rules but I like a lot more than I don't like. I believe it's a system that works.

Leaders or Politicians?

One in a million persons is a true leader. I am hopeful that some of our political representatives are true leaders; however, most of them are politicians or lawyers, people we look for when we're in trouble. The majority of them are elected because they possessed answers and can raise funds. It's not perfect by any means, but I don't have a better idea.

Are you a Republican? Do you follow that party? Are you a Democrat? Are you a Libertarian? Or a Member of the Green Party? Or the Peace and Freedom Party? Do you vote? Do you think it matters? If you don't vote, you don't have a say. Does just your vote, that one vote make a difference? Yes. It makes you part of the solution.

I'm thankful for Freedom. I'm thankful for the beautiful place I live and play and work. I've been a lot of places; the more I travel, the more I realize the nicest place in the world is home. For me, home is here, in California. I love the ocean. I love the freedom I have. As long as you don't cross the double line, nobody bothers you.

Your Time to Lead

Think for your self, follow the right path, lead when it is your time to lead, follow when it is your time to follow. How will you know? You'll feel a push or a nudge — in your heart, in your ideas, in your spirit. Sometimes you will be afraid to step out there. When the invitation to lead comes, go for it. Remember, it's not so important whether you lead or follow, it's walking your path that matters most.

If you have been chosen for Leadership, you will find you will be a leader in sports, in life, with your friends and your family. When others have problems, they will seek your opinion. You'll be there. You will know what to say, how to fix things and how to help people. You will be mentally tough and understand how to create the right balance. You will make friends everywhere. Know you will be blessed.

My Brother, a Leader

As a lad, I willingly followed my brother, he watched out for me. He protected me, he took care of me and I felt safe with him.

I followed him because he knew where he was going. When we got there, it was the right place, it was fun, it tasted good, it made me laugh. He took me to the best places to play and showed me how to play once we got there. If we were playing with others, when he spoke, they listened, they knew from experience that he would be leading us in the right direction. And if one of us messed up, he would straighten it out.

The Broken Window

One day, one of us hit the ball through a window (yeah, it was me — a true story). We all run except my brother. Was he a big dummy? Or was he doing what was right?

He knocked on the door, "I am really sorry but we hit the ball really well and it went through your window, I hope you're not mad, I *wanted* to run, but I knew it wasn't right."

"Well son, did you throw the ball up and hit it by yourself?

Where is everybody else?"

"Well, Ma'am, I don't know. I'm not sure. It's just that the ball went through your window and I felt responsible."

"But who hit the ball?

"I'm not sure. They all followed me here to play. I brought the bat, I brought the ball, I actually told them this was a good place to play. Gosh, I taught them the game. They sort of follow me around.

"I just want to say that I am sorry, I don't have any money to fix your window but if there is anything that I can do to help you, I would really like to make it right."

"Well son, I think you did the right thing. I can take care of the window. I really appreciate you coming to me and not running away like the rest of your friends. You must be the captain of the team.

"Come in and have some cookies and milk, I just got the cookies out of the oven."

"Thank you Ma'am, but do you have enough for my brother and my friends? I think they are out there hiding."

"Of course I do. But you were the only one that came to the door. You took responsibility for something you didn't even do."

"Actually, I did bring them here and I did tell them it was a good place to play. I taught him how to swing the bat and I threw the pitch. Thank you for your offer of the cookies but, if you don't have enough for my brother and my friends — I think I'll have to go and find them. They will be worried and I want to let them know that everything is okay. I'll be by tomorrow. I noticed that your lawn needs mowing. I can do that. I want to do something for you."

Milk and Cookies for Everyone!

"Thank you, son. You're quite a boy. I'm glad you broke my window — I mean, I don't want you to do it again but it was special to meet you. I can see why they followed you here. Go get your friends. I've got enough milk and cookies for everyone."

8

One Pair of Hands

One special person

I've believed that one pair of hands only works for one pair of hands; but, one mind can work for millions of pairs of hands. The truth is I was shallow. I never thought it through. I was belittling the person that was creating or working with one pair of hands, creating something beautiful, special, out of the box. If you make something special with your hands, you make something that inspires and nurtures you and every one who comes in contact with your creation.

One Pair of Hands

One pair of hands, one mind, one special, precious, inspired, passionate, intellectual mind that doesn't just *think* outside the box but *lives* outside the box, can create something so perfect, so passionate, as simple as a thought or a phrase, a painting, a beautiful melody, *Here Comes the Sun — it's alright now.* Each person that comes in contact with it, everyone that sees it, everyone that hears it and feels it will be moved, inspired and changed. Share your creations with your friends and family. *Your two hands with that one special mind touches others and, one by one, changes the world to be a more beautiful place.*

Live Outside the Box

I like the term *think outside the box*; I *love* the term *live outside the box.* In order to create something so passionate, so special, you *must* be a liberated thinker.

"I think the world's round."

"That's ridiculous, everybody knows the world's flat. They've been studying it for years. It's a proven fact."

"Yeah, but I think the world's round."

One person living outside the box. The idea was right. But everybody in his world knew it was wrong. Follow the rules, stay in line, and don't ask questions. Eventually, he believed them.

"They've got to be right. Everyone knows it's a proven fact. I must be really stupid. If the world was round, heck, we'd all fall off! What a dumb idea!"

Einstein, Mozart, Keller, Ghandi and Jordan were all passionate people who created brilliant theories, beautiful melodies, unique communications, messages from God, and played the game shoulders above the rest. These individuals were told by others that what they were doing was wrong, didn't measure up.

That Flow Thing You Do

Einstein flunked out of school and was told his ideas and concepts just didn't hold up. "Nobody's ever going to listen to this music — it's too different; heck, you can't hear, you can't see, you can't speak, you'll never be able to communicate; you can't pull down an empire without an army; that's not fundamental basketball, two-handed chest pass, damn it. Run the plays. *Stay out of that flow thing you do.*"

They were unique individuals who didn't walk in line. Even though others walked familiar paths, they chose another. Even though others told them their paths were wrong — get back in line, follow the leader, don't ask stupid questions — *they followed their path, their passion, their calling.*

Are We All Special?

Are we all special? How did we lose our passion? How did we lose our own identities? What happened? It's popular and safe to agree with others, to go along with their beliefs. Follow the leader, be a good soldier, don't think for yourself, let someone else do it for you. Fall in line. Everybody's doing it. Heck, it's a proven fact, we all know the world is flat.

You Are Special

Those individuals who are known, popular, advertised, shoved in front of our faces are not the most attractive, most intelligent or most spectacular. The truly special persons are all around you! Each one. You! No one is like you. You are special! *You are that one special person to prosper this creation — make it a better place.*

Ever see the movie, *It's a Wonderful Life?* It shows what the world would be like if you were not here? Wow!

One of You

Think for yourself. Believe in yourself. There is only one of you. You are unique, one of a kind. Live outside the box. Just because everybody knows it to be the truth doesn't mean that it is. Those who persevere with passion, will contribute something special to their lives and the lives of others.

Just because the world believes it, adores it, is doing it doesn't mean that it is true or valuable to anyone or the world. If you don't follow the path, you know, the path everybody else follows — stay in line, do what you are told, follow the leader — you will be an individual. You will be you. You are special. Be the person, be that individual that you were created to be, one of a kind, special. You will forge a path that no one else has walked.

When you travel your path, you create something original, something truly yours. You create something for others that changed their path. The path you took was right. It was perfect. It was passionate. It was original.

"Hey this way was wrong, that weirdo showed us the right way. I can't believe I thought it was the right path because everybody said it was. Heck, it was proven to be the right path. I read about it in school. It was a proven fact. I wrote a book report on it, I saw it on TV, read it in the paper. How could everybody have been so wrong?"

It Has to Start With Me

Think for yourself. Believe in yourself. *It's okay to step out of line to step onto your own path.* Follow it. Believe even if nobody else does. Live outside the box; ask questions even if another person thinks your questions are stupid. You will discover your passion and your individuality. Others will see something new, something special, and something original. Others will dare to seek their own path. The world and the people you touch will be inspired.

It doesn't start with you — it has to start with me. It doesn't start with you, it has to start with me. It doesn't start with you. It has to start with me.

You mean, I can think for myself, my ideas are okay? They are not stupid? Okay, maybe some of them are, but one, two, maybe three will be right and they will be yours and inspire you on. Then, the followers can follow you, until someone else decides he or she wants to think for themselves. It doesn't start with you, it has to start with me. That's some really good stuff; read it again, take it to your heart and live it. ***It has to start with me.***

9

Passion

Get it back

We've been learning and growing our whole lives — something new every day. When we first talked about subjects for this book, this topic never came up. But, as we write, we learn; the book writes us. We wondered, without passion, what have you got?

Passion Moves History

We looked up passion in *Webster's Unabridged*. This one phrase out of two whole pages seemed right for us: "passion is that state of being subjected to or acted on by what is external or foreign to one's true nature; a state of desire or emotion that represents the influence of what is external and opposes thought and reason." What does that mean? Let's figure it out!

Opposes thought and reason? Foreign to one's true nature? Umm. Passion bypasses our minds, does not come from thought or reason. It **must** come from within the soul or our inner being. It is spiritual. It comes from the heart.

Passion: Intense feeling. Depth. Affection. Object of desire or interest. Something that commands one's enthusiasm, zeal, intense, overwhelming, driving emotion. Glowing, lasting emotion. Because, it's pure feeling. ***It's powerful. Passion moves history. Passion gets things done.***

Escapes Definition

We're having trouble with an analogy that grasps the essence and power of passion. It's not really something to capture in words. It's bigger than words. It's passion. Whenever we think of something, it's not passionate enough. Life without passion would be like we were just going through the motions. We all know people who portray happiness, joy, love, and yet, it's different if they have passion for joy or love. It brings tears to our eyes, a twinge to our hearts. It's emotion. Pure emotion touches our souls and hearts.

Passion Explodes into Action

Passion explodes into action, into creating, into changing. Can you be good at anything without passion? Good? Maybe. Average? Yes. But to be uniquely creative, you must have passion. I love that word. It feels good to say it. Ever see someone play the piano with passion? They close their eyes — in a different world. Keith Jarrett. Brings tears to your eyes. They love what they're doing. Have you seen the *Phantom of the Opera*? Driven by passion. See Michael Jordan hoop? He plays with passion.

Speaks It's Own Message

Passion is not encouraged; in fact, I think it is discouraged. It scares the meek, the bosses, the teachers; everyone whose goal is to control others. It's such a powerful emotion people are afraid of it because it's so beautiful, so pure and speaks its own message. It's not something *they* can control. It is not something they can emulate.

Passion Squelched

Children are passionate, passionate about everything. And, then, we're told, "Don't cry. Don't laugh so loud. Don't ask stupid questions. Grow up. Act like an adult." So much criticism — we're hurt over and over again. Throughout our lives, we're taught to keep our schedules, be there on time, be dependable and to be controllable. We become afraid to share and show our inner souls, our beings.

Can't Fake Passion

Whenever I'm moved, truly moved, it's by something with great passion. Whenever I hear the song, *"I'd Do Anything For You Mean Everything to Me"*, I feel passion. My Mom sang this to me. It's our song. She sings it with passion.

Passion is something you can't create or learn. You can't study to be passionate. When somebody is truly passionate about what they are doing, it is expression at a completely different level. Passion is beauty in action. Passion is perfect love, not something you can fake or buy. It is real.

Children Are Passionate

Deep Calling to Deep

Passion is one of the most valuable qualities a person can possess. You can't buy it. You can't pretend you have it. You're either passionate or you're not. I think everyone is passionate about something. I *hope* everyone is passionate about something. If we have passion for a subject and they don't, whatever that action is, when we do it, it's passionate; when they do it, they're just doing it. Ever attend a concert and been truly moved? You could go to a concert and see technically the best musicians in the world, but they didn't play with passion; go to another concert with people that wrote their music, felt their music in their hearts, loved to share it with you. They're sharing a piece of their soul. That concert conveys a completely different intensity. They wouldn't have to be the best musicians in the world; they played with great passion.

Passion reaches in to touch your heart. It's deep. It has depth. It conveys something deep, deeper than words, more profound than feeling. ***Deep calling to deep.***

Passion Transforms

I've had many coaches; some good, some bad. Some knew everything about coaching, but had no passion. Coach Jerry McGowan and Coach Bob Enzweiler loved us, loved me, loved the game. They coached with passion. It's a completely different world. Passion transforms. I loved to go to practice. I loved listening to them. I loved to please them. They knew about the flow. They were passionate. I was passionate with them. It's a whole other world, another level. It's inspirational. We play with heart for them. I'm passionate about basketball. I love the game. It's my therapy. When I'm there, there's nothing there except me, the ball, the rim, my teammates and the opponents. I don't think. I react. I play with passion. It's a perfect flow.

All Those Red Marks

When I was young, I loved to write. I was passionate about it. I lost my passion for writing. They said I couldn't spell, the punctuation was wrong, my grammar sucked. I've been learning to write on the computer.

My brother sent me a laptop. It's got these little green or red zigzags under the word depending on whether it's spelling or grammar.

"Richard, I feel like I'm doing something wrong. All those red marks — reminds me of school; I want to fix it."

"Wait until you get to the end before you correct all the bad stuff."

I realized it's the reason I quit writing. I was ashamed of my penmanship, and my spelling. I had great stuff to put down on paper but I didn't want everybody to think I was unintelligent because of my creative writing skills!

Wings of Passion

Does a person really **have** passion? Of course, but you can't hold it or call it up whenever you want. Passion is something that favors you with its presence. It might visit you when you're doing something **with all of your heart.**

We all know people who show passion — in the way they cook, the way they sing, the way they dance. Ever had a passionate hug? You know the one. You held each other for a long time. Neither wanted to let go. Passion. It's perfect. It's beautiful. It's life. It's true love. It's sharing something that's special. It carries poetry, history, truth, love and all things noble on its wings.

Passion Sells

Where do we see passion? Hollywood. They sell passion. They make a movie about it. What would it be without passion? What would a love story be without passion? Have you seen *The Godfather?* Passion, brutal, raw, brilliant passion. The people who wrote this movie were passionate about it, the people who acted in this movie were passionate about it. What about *Rudy?* Did you see that movie? If you haven't, watch it. *Rudy* had passion. Every time I see that movie, I cry; I've seen it 20 times.

Starving For Passion

Is that true passion when we sit there and watch it? No. It's not. But, we're starving for passion, even if it is someone else's. We sit and watch and watch, hoping some will seep into us. We need to grasp our own passion; we all need to be more passionate. It's okay to be passionate. It's okay to cry. It's okay to feel. It's okay to love. It is being truly alive. It's rejoicing in life. It's celebrating.

Richard's Beautiful Birds

When my brother was a child, he was passionate about art. He drew beautiful birds. He drew one of these birds for a class at school. When he showed it

to his teacher, they made red marks all over it, told him what was wrong with it and gave him a "D" grade. I still remember his face and the raw pain in it. He said his teacher said the bird wasn't "right". He lost his passion for drawing beautiful birds.

No matter what we write on these pages, we can't express passion adequately with words. Passion is passion.

Even a Spark

I got my passion back. I'm so passionate about writing. What were you passionate about? Whatever it was, get it back! Even a spark. Follow it. It's your path. Find your passion. Nurture passion. When you sense passion, love it, embrace it, fan it like a spark or an ember. Turn it into a bonfire. Passion is life. Live it. Say this with me, say it with love and meaning: PASSION, PASSION, PASSION, PASSION. I'M PASSIONATE. I FEEL YOUR PASSION. I LIVE LIFE WITH PASSION. LOVE WITH PASSION. PLAY WITH PASSION. WORK WITH PASSION.

PARENT WITH PASSION.

10

——

Parent Time Out

No one has all the colors

ig Mark is going through a tough time with a divorce. He loves his children Sherrie and Mark and wants to be with them. They want to be with him and their mother too. Big Mark is right next to me. He tells his story with tears in his eyes.

"Not to tuck them in at night, you know, kiss them and hold them and make sure they are okay. Not just physically, but ask them how their day was, talk to them and hold them, hear them, father them, be with them, father and child. Help them with their worries or fears. And tell them,

'I love you more than anything in the universe.
Sweet dreams. I will see you in the morning.'
Adam, it breaks my heart."

Problems Got Worse

Mark and his wife have been trying to work things out for the last three years. Their problems worsened. Their relationship is over as husband and wife, but not as parents.

Both are thankful for their children. The precious gift of their children is what the hurt is about. They don't want to lose that gift. When they realized their relationship was over, they began fighting for their right to be parents. The problem was, most of the fighting was going on through their kids (ouch!).

Fighting Through the Kids

I don't remember my parents being together, but I do remember them fighting. I always took Mom's side and identified with her world; my brother took my Dad's side. Richard has a different relationship with my Father. He is more responsible and has a great work ethic. Richard moved to live with him because he thought that was right. He left me. It still hurts. He was my voice, my leader, my role model. He is my best friend, my big brother. I missed him. Mom was heart broken when Richard left. Each person suffered hurt.

It's His Fault. No, It's Her Fault

When parents divorce, each parent is hurt and wants sympathy. What do they do? The parent pressures the children to take sides, their side! Each parent wants to believe he or she is right, that each is good and honest, that he or she was not responsible for the problems.

"It is his fault."

"No, Son, it was her fault because, etc. etc. etc."

The children believe both of them. After all, it is their Mom and Dad! Eventually, they pick a side.

If the parents were sensible adults, they would find the courage to be honest with their children.

Mark interrupts Adam, "Stop, I need you to put this in for me.

"Adam, listen. You're always telling me change is inevitable, growth is optional. The truth is, we want our children to love us. We want to be perfect for them. We don't want them to see our failures. We hide from them."

I am thinking Mark is really a great father. He is crying. He's about to come clean.

"You're right Adam. I'm guilty of trying to get my children to take my side."

Mark opens up with tears and says, "I am learning. My mind and spirit are changing. I just didn't want to see it. We should be real with ourselves and our children."

Telling the Truth

The reality is we're all human. We all make mistakes. Mark resolves to tell his kids, "Your mother is a wonderful person. I will always love her and she will always love me. We have both made mistakes. We don't know how to get along as husband and wife. We have decided to separate. We are thankful for the most beautiful gift we have ever been given — you two kids. We will always love you as your Mother and Father."

When is a child old enough to hear the truth? When should a father or mother lie to their kids to protect them from a bigger hurt? Only when it suits their needs???!!!

Be the person you want your child to be. Role model. Role model. Role model. Whose fault is it? It's your fault. It's their fault. It's our fault. It's my fault.

It has to start with you, no, not you, me. Take responsibility. You can make it better. Who knows? Maybe, we would all be healed!

Does It Make You Happy to Think That Way?

Dwell on the good. Dwell on the beauty. Find it. It's there. Seek it out. Want the truth. Stop building your case. It's so much better to be happy. We have a choice. What should we chose? Let's think about it together. "Let's see. Do I want to be happy? Or complain? Good? Or, bad? Can I be a better parent, role model, husband, wife, mate, ex-husband, ex-wife, friend, person?"

What do you chose? You have a choice. Make it. It really is just that simple. It's the first day of the rest of your life. What do you chose?

THIS IS MOM. ADAM INVITED ME TO INCLUDE SOME PARENTING CONCEPTS FOR YOU.

No One But You

That baby, with her unique personality and special gifts was sent to you. Look upon your child as if you have been assigned to carry out a divine task. You have. To do this everyday, with humor, good will, shopping, cooking, cleaning and cleaning and cleaning will transform you into a Saint. No one but you, the parent, can do this.

Your Heartbeat

You were chosen to receive this precious gift. Hold her. Rock him. They want *you.* Babies are meant to be held. That's why they can't walk! Naked next to your skin — skin to skin, heart to heart. Your heartbeat comforts him — that's why it's there! You will look back at this baby time as being — oh so dear.

Meant to be Held

The Drama Shift

Life changes dramatically when you become a parent. You are no longer the most important person in your world. This little one has swapped places with you. It's the great drama shift.

See the Good

Your child desires to please you. He wants you to think she is wonderful! See how good your child is. See how beautiful he is, her spirit, her joy, his unique personality. Allow your child to delight you with her being. Give that child your best stuff, your most wholesome caring, your open, loving, laughing, joyful self. See the good in that child.

Give your attention to what the child does that is wonderful! *Don't even notice what is missing the mark.* Don't even sense the bad stuff — pour your approval out over the many, many positive behaviors of your child.

Beauty

Surround your child with beauty. It has been documented that children who hear classical music (maybe Mozart?) develop increased intelligence. Play lovely, classical music. Put kind, beautiful pictures in his room, the Madonna with the Child, pictures that soothe the emerging soul.

You Fathers

You have been chosen to care for this child, to love the mom. You are *very* important and help the mom so much. At times, she will be exhausted. Your quiet, loving strength brings vitality to her. When you love her, you nurture your child.

The Supreme Teacher — Modeling

Your child learns through you. He watches you like a hawk. She sees everything you do — every expression, every reaction, every movement. They soak you in. If you want your child to be a certain way, *be* that way. Live, act, and move as if you were teaching your child with your being. You are.

Blue Marbles

In the story of Irv from *Bring Something to the Party,* you'll meet the father with different colored marbles in his pocket. His son wanted so much for his father to give him a blue marble. Irv fell over and all the marbles rolled out. Irv didn't have a blue marble. No matter how sorely the son wanted or perhaps needed that blue marble — Irv just didn't have it!

Your child wants certain colored marbles from you. *No one has all the colors.* So, what to do? You do your best. You can't be *all things* to your child. Following are some basics that will provide a solid foundation.

"Don't Hit Johnny"

Model what you believe. If you want your child to be kind, be kind; if you want your child to be honest, be honest; if you want your child to be brave, be brave. Be what you want the child to become.

If you hit your child, then, say, "Don't hit Johnny." That you hit and tell the child not to hit is creased into the child's mind and memory. "Okay, Mom says not to hit and she hits me — I guess that means when you are grown you can hit your child and tell your child not to hit other children." Think about it.

The Boob Tube

The worst thing in our lives and in our children's lives other than war, graft, greed, murder, lies and corruption is television. Adam thinks this statement is too strong. He said, "It's wonderful to come home when you're tired, turn the tube on and relax — just go brain dead."! It might be all right for a grown up, but for a child? The child between the ages of birth and seven soaks in all that she witnesses. Please, think of the terrible stuff on television! Movies, television with murder, rape, slashing etc., are not for your young one to witness. I would say, they are not even for you to witness. ("Oh, Mom!")

Think about it: first, the programs are usually awful; second, what are they (or you) getting out of sitting, watching people do things. Why not, instead, be about living? When Daddy comes home from work, make a snack, crackers and peanut butter, sit under a tree and look at the clouds. Go for a walk with your child.

Collect leaves, bugs, grasses. Sort, catalog, paint them. They need to do, to be about living.

Get Off Our Duffs

In olden times, children helped the parents. The boys worked with the dad and the girls with the mother. They learned by doing and they learned by watching. They were with their parents.

What does this mean to us? We have to get off our duffs and make things for them to do. We set out activities, teach them to clean up and do it together. This is the natural way for children to learn. Don't drive yourself crazy with this; find a rhythm, plan ahead, make it work for you.

Home School?

Ever wonder why or how home schooled children perform better than kids in public school? Presumably, teachers have been educated and trained to produce learning in the child. Parents are better teachers *because they <u>love</u> the child.* There is a power in love that transcends teacher training.

Foundations

There are three things you can do that will see your child through any blitz!

They are:

> Listen
>
> Be Yourself
>
> Be Honest

When you listen (relax, breathe, focus), you will connect with your child. Be open and sincere, you'll be yourself. The child will trust you and feel safe. The third is to be honest, tell the truth, they can count on you. Your child arrives listening, being his/herself and being honest. Be like your child in these ways.

Listening Solves Problems

Listening solves most problems. Listening allows the other person/child to share thoughts and feelings. After they communicate precious parts of themselves to an understanding listener, they usually know what to do next. Please, don't let them pour their heart out and then *tell them what to do!!!* If they want your solutions, *wait until they ask you*; otherwise, let them figure it out. That's the way they learn!

Listening Heals

The following exercise has been repeated over and over and over and the result is *always* the same. I've asked people to recall a time when someone listened to them and remember the feelings they had. And here are their answers: *love, important, excited, cared about, like I can do it, energized.*

I've also asked people to recall a time when someone didn't listen to them and remember the feeling they had. And here are their answers: *unloved, unimportant, rejected, not cared about, sad, angry, defeated, discouraged.* Your listening is healing to your child and others around you. When listening, set aside the desire to control and the custom of telling others what to do. Become humble, kind, caring and focused. It's good for us to listen. Do it. I am so proud of you!

Being Yourself

Being yourself means we can see right through you! After you've spent all that energy hiding yourself, now, we want you to open that self up. Be real, be sincere. When you stop hiding, you save a lot of energy and you allow other people to see you. It's pretty challenging but you will be your simple, beautiful, wonderful, unhurried, true self. Turn one way. Turn another. Nothing hidden here. You're a miracle!

Keep Your Promises

Don't make a promise you are not going to keep. Tell the truth. Keep your word. Don't placate your child. Don't be phony and tell her what you *think* she wants to hear. Be honest. Be real. They can take that a lot better than a hundred disappointments. Tell the truth. Say, "I'd really like to do that with you, but I won't promise right now."

Cry, Daddy, Cry!

If you feel sad and your child asks you, "What's the matter, Mom? Or Dad?" Don't say "Nothing." Say, "I'm feeling sad." Tell the truth. If you share your feelings, your child will share his feelings. Know that feelings are processed — on the move.

Dad, you, too. Let those tears flow. You have had a lot of pressure put on you to stop the natural flow of tears. It's tough, I know. As much as you can, let your tears come out. Cry, Daddy, cry!

Violence

Want a violent child? Try, "Stop crying or I'll give you something to cry about." Shut off those tears with threat, fear and anger and you'll raise a child whose pain is blocked as they contrive to develop a demeanor that won't get them beat up by their parent.

(There's the mask.) *Every* violent man in prison had witnessed violence as a child, *every one, one hundred percent.* They didn't *invent* violence; they *learned* violence.

Parents, children learn what is happening. Let your philosophy and your teaching fit your living. Want a kind, caring child. Be kind and caring. Comfort the child's pain.

Out of that Rough Sea

Love isn't being "in love" although that brings you together. After the in love part wanes, and it will, real loving starts. You are kind, helpful, patient, thinking good of the other, doing good for the other. If you wait it out, rough seas calm and your marriage improves.. You love each other more. You are both more kind and appreciative. Both of you are right. Be forgiving. Be good, be kind, be loving, be patient. Be gentle and sweet. Your actions can change everything.

So, instead of fighting and raising the barriers, smash them down with love; he will melt, she will melt. Grab that tiller that takes you, your spouse and family out of that rough sea and into grace. You can do it. You choose to do it. You are SO powerful!

Growing the Kids

A loving, steady home grows kids. What are they learning if you are fighting (wanting your own way — selfishness), threatening to leave (being a quitter), disrespectful of one another (harshness, unkindness)? You are teaching them selfishness, quitting when things are hard and to be unkind and harsh.

I couldn't resist passing on this one lesson to you. It is a perfect solution to the temper tantrum.

Aggressive Comforting

This is an amazing solution for the true temper tantrum. *Only do this if you can commit the time.* It doesn't work if you stop too soon. It might take 30 minutes.

Hold the child firmly so he/she can't hurt you. Rhythmically rock her and croon repeatedly, "I love you, I won't let anything hurt you, I won't let you hurt yourself, I love you, Daddy (Mommy) loves you, Gammy loves you." Repeat this over and over and over, holding the child firmly all the while. Don't let her hurt you. You might have to restrain him.

Continue in this mode (***don't give up!***) until, suddenly, the child takes a deep, beautiful breath and totally wilts in your arms. He may then sob in a different kind of way. Rock and tell this valiant warrior you love him/her. The child will go to sleep in your arms.

Education — Drawing Forth

Kids learn through discovery. They flower. There are times when certain learning blossoms. If we try to open a flower at the wrong time, we pull out the petals and injure the flower. The child needs to flower ***from the inside out***, growing at her own pace and interest, not fitting into some pre-designed curriculum — or lectures!

Activities and Rhythms

Adam's sister Jerilee, a magnificent parent, shares her wisdom.

The teenager, while striving to become a separate individual, is still a child. He needs to be respected and cared for at the same time. Parents need to establish healthy rhythms for the child, interspersed with activities. This is the time to sign them up for music lessons, tennis lessons, etc. Keep them busy.

Teens Sensitive

Your teen is overly sensitive about your opinion. He is sometimes unreasonable. Proceed with caution! Be sensitive, respectful and strong. There is an art to discern when to say what. You can do it. Be quiet, listen, search for the right words and the right time. Be an artist. You have it in you. I know you do!

Spend Time With Teens

Be with your teenager as much as they allow you to be with them. If they ask you to stay up and watch a movie 'til two, do it. If they ask you to go to the beach or go to a concert, go. Jerilee says she's been to

Bee Keepers

four *Dave Matthews* concerts. If they want their friends to come over or they want you to go somewhere with their friends, go. Enjoy their friends. Include them in your family. Do as much with them as possible. Enjoy, or at least share their music. Be interested in their classes, what they are studying.

Pour Yourself Out

Mom speaking again. At a recent memorial for Rhonda, young, college age men shared. They spoke of Rhonda and Richard warmly welcoming them into their home: for snacks, dinners, swimming and parties. They emphasized how much this meant to them during their high school days. You never know the degree you are helping as you pour yourself out for those kids.

Jerilee and Laddy

Mom and the Home

The keeper of the home is the most important, most influential task you will ever have. You sculpt and design the home, that place your husband comes every day after work, that nest that nurtures, raises and produces your wonderful children. You will get no credit, will not be admired nor acknowledged. But, know that the power is *yours!*

The home is created by your loving heart. This is more important than "bringing home the bacon" (notice where the 'bacon' comes to!) — more important than earning a doctorate, being in Congress, being a doctor, being a star of one sort or another. This home reflects your heart. It refreshes your husband and yourself and grows your children. A wonderful woman. Blessing the world with your special wisdom!

The Three L's Dad

You are so important! You love and appreciate the mother, your wife. You nurture and guide your children. *Your little girls will pick a man like you to marry!* Think of that! How very important you are. Be the kind of man you want your daughter to pick out — to marry — to be the father of *your* grandchildren! Be steady, patient and kind. Be fun, happy and helpful. Love, and adore your wife. They will bask in the hot tub of your love! It nourishes them and

Rhonda

Rich

teaches them to be a husband and father. Kids usually naturally adore the Dad. Use the adoration to wisely guide them on paths of goodness.

Many men think they have to always be right, that being right is manly. Give that up. Replace it with honesty. Work things out. If we think we are always right, how are we ever going to learn anything? Be open. Listen, Learn. Love. Hey, the three LLL's: listen, learn, love. Be that kind of Dad, the Three LLL'S Dad.

11

Time

It's all yours

When we hear the truth, we know it. Check this out. The most amazing, powerful, precious gift we are blessed with is that we choose what to do with the time we are given. We can do whatever we want and we can be whoever we want to be — not just dream about it but live it. We can think our thoughts, choose our words and control our actions.

Time is Life

What time is it? It's time to start worrying about the future! What is "the future"? An imaginary concept of time — out there somewhere? It's time to enjoy the time we have. Right now! Our time is short and getting shorter. There's no dress rehearsals.

Time to Complain

Some people are negatively obsessed with time. David was on vacation, buying a fish burger. There was a guy in line in front of him who started a stopwatch on his wrist. While he was in line, he complained about the 22 minutes it took to get his burger. He complained how they wasted his time.

Dave was sitting in a chair next to him. He made friends with the most beautiful little girl. She was three years old. Her name was Laurie. Her parents didn't want to go swimming, so David went swimming with Laurie and had the greatest 22 minutes waiting for his burger.

When Dave left, the anxious gentleman was swearing about how long it took to prepare his hamburger and that he only had 63 hours left on Maui! Was Maui glad when he left? Maybe.

Time is Life — the LifeTime!

Time is life. Time is the time we spend in our lifetime. Our Lifetime. Do you ever think about that lifetime? Spend your time wisely. You've heard it said, "I wasted all that time." Another person might say, "It was tough, but I learned so much during that time." Or, "I had the time of my life, it was all good."

A Bad or a Good Time?

When you think of the "good old days", were they a bad or a good time? That time of your life is past. It's gone. It's over. You can think about the good things. You can think about the sunsets, your family, that special person. You can picture the way she looked when she saw you, how much she enjoyed being with you, what a great lifetime she had. You have a choice. What do you choose??

Do you ever throw a party, and wonder if they had a good time? Did they enjoy their time with us? Really? That was up to them. I think, "They had a great time and I had a great time."

Make Your Time Count

My Pop says life is about creating memories, memories that nurture and warm your heart. Time is short. Time waits for no one. Dwell on the good times; learn from the bad times. Start enjoying your time now. You have a choice. It's just that simple. I might as well enjoy my time. Did I help people during my time here? Was I a positive influence?

Make your time here count. What time is it? It's the best time in my life. Right now. This second. Yesterday's gone. Tomorrow's uncertain. The only reality is right now, right now, right now. I might as well enjoy this time, right now. I'm having the time of my life right now, this second. There's still time to change!

The Bad Times Teacher

If I could change something in my life, would I? Guess what? That time's past. We enjoy the good times; we learn from the bad times. They teach us. They are our best instructor. Don't change the past. It's over — gone. If you must focus on the bad times, get something good out of your concentration. How do you know it was bad? What did you learn? In any situation, you can find some good;

you can learn from it. We've all had hard times. We've all had good times. There's still time to change!

Dance So Fast

If you were one of the unfortunate people that didn't get touched and you saw it but you didn't see it; you heard it but you didn't hear it. You were there, you were right in front of it, you looked at it, but you never felt it, this might be for you.

> "Have you ever watched kids on a merry-go-round
> or listened to the rain lapping on the ground?
> Ever follow a butterfly's erratic flight
> or gazed at the sun into the fading night?
>
> "You better slow down, don't dance so fast
> Time is short. The music won't last.
> Do you run through each day on the fly?
> When you ask, 'How are you?', Do you hear the reply?
> When the day is done, do you lie in your bed
> With the next hundred chores running through your head?
>
> "You better slow down, don't dance so fast
> Time is short. The music won't last.
>
> "Ever told your child 'We'll do it tomorrow'
> And in your haste, not see their sorrow?
> Ever lost touch. Let a good friendship die
> Cause you never had time to call and say 'Hi'?
>
> "When you run so fast to get somewhere
> You miss the fun of getting there.
> When you worry and hurry through your day
> It is like an unopened gift...thrown away...

"Life is not a race. Take it slower.
Hear the music. Before the song is over.
Life is short. Enjoy it while you can."

(Anonymous pre-teen stricken with terminal cancer)

Maybe you were in a hurry; it might have been worth experiencing. What do you think, Genius?

Start now. What have you got to lose? It's just that simple. What time is it? It's your Best Day Ever. Be successful.

12

Faith

Faith, prove it!

Life, death, good, bad, forgiveness, heaven, hell, right, wrong, faith, assumptions, reality? So many questions with so many different answers. No, not answers, opinions.

"I desperately need some concrete facts. What is real? What is reality?"

What's the Truth, Please?

Are these the truth: pictures, a movie, a true-life experience? Wait a minute. I've seen pictures, watched movies, documentaries and embraced true-life experiences. What is reality? I want to believe. I do believe.

"Well, I'm pretty sure — but, well, what if — please, can somebody tell me the truth?"

Without a Shadow of a Doubt

Wait a minute. Everywhere I look, I see differing answers to every question — every impression I've ever pondered is answered. It's the truth — without a shadow of a doubt. I've read books that had all the right answers; I've watched true-to-life documentaries on TV. They've got to be true, haven't they? Oops, right next to it was another book, another documentary telling me without a shadow of a doubt that just the opposite was the truth.

The movies, the documentaries, they are absolutely positive they are right. Everything I perceive as the truth turns out to be a farce, a lie. They're so convincing. The world is flat. Everybody knows it's a proven fact. I saw it on TV. I read it in the paper. I learned it in school. Without a shadow of a doubt, it is the truth. Everybody knows it.

I'm not sure what to believe. Can anyone please tell me the truth? Everyone has answers but, the more I search, the more I realize each person's answers are different.

Have a Little Faith

Have a little faith. Wow! What a concept. Faith, hummmm, faith.

Can someone tell me what to have faith in? Stop. Too much input. Every place I investigate produces a different solution. "You have to have faith in this. No, not this. This. My faith is the only way to salvation." I don't know what to believe, what to have faith in. I wish I could know with certainty, make a definite decision and put my faith into that.

Wait a minute. I can make decisions. I can actually choose. I do know right from wrong. I have faith. Prove it. I know without question, one hundred percent positive that my Mom loves me. Prove it. **Faith**. It's the absolute truth for me. It's mine. It's the truth for me, not for you.

It's real. I can take a picture of it.

"See. There it is. It's so obvious. See, the way she looks, the love she feels for me is right there in front of you in living color. It's obvious."

I might be able to talk you into it — tell you how positive my faith is, how right my faith is, how honest, how truthful. Even if you believe me and it becomes your faith, there's no way you will feel it, experience that undeniable love. That love that is real, true, and honest, without question.

It's Just the Truth

It's the **truth**. But, because it's the truth for me doesn't make it the truth for you. It's not real for you. You will never know it as I know it. Does that make it **not** the truth just because you don't see it or feel it as I do?

"What do you mean you can't see it? It's the truth. Don't you have any faith?"

Without faith, what do we have? Can you prove tomorrow will come? That the sun will rise, then set again? No. But I believe it will happen. I have faith. It's the truth. Prove it.

The Great Spirit

My faith is strong today. The Great Spirit reached out and touched me. I am so blessed. The Great Spirit knows my potential. Today, I feel the faith the Great Spirit has in me.

"Karma is a Bitch"

I was talking to Jeff a couple of days ago. We chatted about this and that.

"Jeff, I saw my baby's heartbeat, seven weeks old."

"Adam, Kevin is really sick."

I giggled and said, "Yeah. Karma is a bitch."

We both laughed.

"Adam, call Kev. You probably won't get through. I keep telling them I'm Steve (Kev's brother). I still can't get through but you can at least leave him a message."

"Kev, I Heard You Were Dying"

Kevin and I are best friends. Neither knows why. It's a relationship that transcends thought or reality. He knows me and loves me anyway. And I know him and love him. We don't talk about it. It's just there. It's real. It's the truth. I have faith in him — he has faith in me. No one else can feel it, much less, understand it. I can't begin to put it into words.

Anyway, I picked up the phone and gave him a call.

"Hello. Hello, Kev?"

"Ya, who is it?"

"It's Goldie. I heard you were dying so I thought I'd give you a call."

"I can't believe it's you. I haven't answered the phone in ten days."

"I heard they took your gall bladder out. What's a gall bladder?"

I Saw This Guy, John —

"It filters the bad stuff out of your blood. Mine has been messed up for over a year. I've been treating it with wheat grass and acupuncture. I thought it was healed. It's been hurting for a while but, you know, Goldie, we have a great tolerance for pain. Remember all those games with sprained ankles — black and blue, as big as a grapefruit? I kept putting it off.

"It started hurting really bad so I went to my acupuncturist. He put one needle in. The pain was unbearable so I went straight to the hospital.

"I saw this guy, John —"

Kev starts to get really emotional. He begins to cry, just a little at first.

"God, I love John. He saved my life. Anyway, they took my gall bladder out. I was supposed to go home that night. About one in the morning, I started bleeding, coughing up blood. It was coming out of my ears, my mouth, and my butt. They called John, at one in the morning. He answered. He told them to take me to ICU (intensive care unit). I thought, 'What if John was sick? What if he didn't answer?' I could have died.'"

At this point, we were both sobbing.

"I thought I was going to die. John came. I was laying on the gurney. He said, 'This is really serious.' He stuck this camera thing up through my belly button and saw that I had an ulcer that had eaten through my stomach and right through one of my main arteries. John saved my life. I died and he brought me back."

He's sobbing. I'm sobbing.

Kev, Did You See God?

"Kev, did you see God?"

Kev starts crying uncontrollably.

"I haven't told anybody about it. I don't want to minimize the experience. Don't tell Jeff or Boo. I don't want everybody talking about it.

We're Going to Battle

"It's mine. It changed my life. I saw God. I was bathed in white Light. I was dressed in a gladiator's outfit. He put His Hand on my head and told me, 'We're going to battle tonight.' The next thing I remember I was talking to Rachel.

"Goldie, I am so blessed. I love my wife and my kids. Rachel told me the first thing I said when I woke up was, 'We went to battle tonight.' God touched me and gave me another chance."

"It's no longer an assumption. There is a God and He saved a wretch like me and, yes, we are forgiven. I'm going to be so much better. Wow. Faith. Faith, I love you, Goldie."

"I love you too, Kev. I've never been more proud of you."

Truth is Real

This is a true story. If Kev is forgiven and, if he is, we all have a chance. How powerful this is. Everywhere we look, we see and feel peoples' passionate legends. Their truth.

Truth's not just a story, a show, a movie. Truth is real. Believe what you want. It's your choice. Believe. When we hear the truth, we know the Truth.

Have a little faith.

13

The True Friend

On our side

Making friends is so important to our happiness. Say "Hello." Ask their names. Make pleasant conversation. Tell jokes. "What did the fish say when it ran into the wall? Damn!" Friends are an incredible blessing.

On Our Side

What is it about those persons that is special, that allows you to love or care for them? And, in turn, causes them to love or care for you? What is it that enables you to confide in him or her — someone to call when you're hurt or need advice?

A true friend is somebody who knows you and loves you anyway. Somebody you can talk to about anything, someone who truly listens. A friend is someone we miss. A friend is someone who calls you even if you haven't seen or talked to them for a year and, instantly, you connect, as if you have never been separated. A friend is someone you can confide in. A friend is someone you can tell something about yourself, something bad, something good, either one, and the friend doesn't judge you. A true friend helps you. They forgive. They love, comfort, advise and they're usually on our side.

Trust

We are all judgmental. When we make a judgment about others, we are holding ourselves above and looking down on them. We're right, they're wrong. We're good, they're bad. A true friend realizes the reason you are sharing that painful experience or letting them see the "real" you is trust. You trust them to understand you and to give caring advice. A friend is someone who knows you and loves you anyway. A friend accepts you for who you are.

Out of Their Way

A friend is someone we can talk to, we can listen to, share good times and bad times. A friend is that person who forgives us. A friend is that person we forgive.

Friends are one of the biggest blessings in our lives. Friends are an extension of who we are. Some people have one or two friends. What is it about that person that is special, that makes you love or care about them? Makes them someone you can confide in — call when you're hurt, call when you need advice? You know that if you need them, they'll be there with whatever you need.

A friend is somebody we count on when we need help or advice, someone we know will go out of their way to come into our way to help us out — that Bridge over troubled water. You know what I am talking about.

Stabbed in the Heart

As your lifetime goes along, you'll find some people are adversaries or take a stance that's different from yours because they can't stand to be close or they have to control. These people don't trust you and, probably, don't trust anyone. Why is that? Because they're scared. They're afraid to trust because they've been hurt. Someone has hurt them. At some time when they were trusting, that special other person stabbed them in the heart. They built a wall after that. They don't want to be hurt again. It is so painful to have trusted and loved someone and to have that person betray that trust and that love.

Relationship Failure

John was in a relationship for several years. His girlfriend Jane was intelligent, attractive, caring, trustworthy, a good partner and a good listener. After two years, they weren't sure they wanted to continue to be together. They wanted to take some time to figure it out. They separated, agreeing that they didn't want to be with anyone else; rather, thinking over what each wanted to do. Just about this time, John learned that his lifelong best friend Scott had been having an affair with Jane for over a year.

When she decided she wanted to be with Scott (best friend), John desperately wanted her back; he got to the point where he was almost groveling, and came really close to having a physical altercation with Scott.

Was It Her? Was It Me?

He was betrayed by his two best friends. Over the next month, every time I saw John, he was dwelling on the hurt and disappointment of the betrayal and was so bitter and angry that when he talked about it, my heart hurt.

"John, what was the reason you were originally thinking about breaking up. What was that about?"

"Adam, I had a hunch she was being deceitful and not always honest. Well, maybe, I messed up and she just might be the right woman for me."

Clear Your Mind and Use Your Head!

"John, clear your mind and use your head. How could she be the right person if you thought she was deceitful and she was; you thought she might be dishonest and she was? And you learned that she'd been deceiving you for over a year?"

Were either of these people friends to John? When you think of it with a clear mind and realize that John could have gone on with this broken relationship, it was a blessing, painful though it was, that he discovered the truth. John could have made a lifelong commitment with Jane and she would have continued to be deceitful and hurtful and dishonest. John was saved a greater hurt.

A Flawed Relationship

"John, you were definitely saved a greater hurt. Think about it. The reason you were breaking up in the first place is because it wasn't a right relationship. The minute you learned that she was with someone else, you shifted your attitude and started thinking about the good times, the great things she did, the way she held you, how beautiful she was." It is human nature to think about the good times when we are out of the situation and nothing is pulling or pushing us.

"It is much more constructive and truthful to think about the real reasons you didn't want to be with her. As a matter of fact, dwell on them. It will take away some of the hurt."

Scott and Jane were married. They had two children. Scott found out that he was not the father of their second child. In a way, the whole episode, even though very painful, produced a positive outcome for John.

Still Bitter

John is still bitter with both of them. Should he forgive them?

"John are you perfect? Have you made terrible mistakes? If you don't forgive them, that pain and those memories remain a part of you; it will be part of your next relationship; it will be part of your friendship with new persons. The bitterness affects your relationships with both men and women. You built a wall. You didn't want to get hurt again. You don't want to trust again. You let this affect you and hurt you and, in your day-to-day life, you became bitter and distrustful, causing your friendships to be shallow."

A Deep Scar

John should sit down with both of these people that he loves and cares for. He needs to tell them how he feels, cry with them, share his hurt and disappointment. He didn't know if he could trust them with this tender openness. If he had done this, it would have helped him. It would have helped him be a better person, a better mate, a better friend. He still carries it around in his day-to-day life. He still mentions it when someone is engaged or in love. It left a deep scar.

How does it help him to hold onto this pain? Maybe the right response is to feel sorry for both of them. If he forgave them, releasing the pain in his heart, not telling them what terrible people they were, but forgave them, and forgave himself, this one act would have made them all better people, better lovers, and better friends. It would have healed them. And, in some small way, heal the hurting world because they're always two sides to every story and every fight.

Best Friends Again?

Maybe, they would be best friends again. Because we're all just doing our best. We all mess up every day. Choose the good. Choose to love. Choose to forgive. Choose not to carry around bad feelings. Choose to fix it now! Choose to get over it. Choose to be a better person.

Forgive and Love Again

We might think, "How can I ever forgive someone who was this hurtful? I don't like them, as a matter of fact, I hate them." Someone who can hurt you this bad is someone you love. Go. Mend that relationship. Forgive them. Forgive yourself. Let it go. Move on with your life. Allow yourself to love again. Allow yourself to trust. Yeah, you'll probably be hurt again. But, that's life. We all mess up. We're just doing our best. Forgive and love again.

John, Jane and Scott

By the way, I went to see John. I called Jane and Scott, now divorced, talked to them about what happened and how it hurt my friend John. I invited them over to my house. I told them to park at the bottom of the hill. I invited John as well. I don't think he would have come if he knew they were going to be there. They all made up. They all cried. They all hugged. John said it was one of the best days of his life.

Scott and John are best friends again. John plays with Jane's kids. We all mess up. We're just doing our best. Forgive. I don't think we forget, but we learn and we learn and we learn.

When to Part Ways?

Do you give up when you realize the person behind the mask is more bad and evil than positive and good? Do you give up when the relationship is killing your spirit, darkening your heart? Is that the time to leave? Is that the time to break up? Cut them off? Time to change? I'm never sure. I think about this a lot. I have friends who are getting a divorce, having problems with their jobs, their children, their parents and they come for advice. The decision to end a relationship is one you must ultimately make on your own. You are the only one who knows the path to take.

When is it time to leave? When is it time to give up? Is it when somebody does something terrible to us? Cheating on us? A terrible lie? It's still a decision you must make on your own. Realize that, most of the time, we cheated on them as well. We told lies that were terrible lies. We know about them. They don't.

Parting? Don't Look Back

Once you see the truth about yourself and the other and you make your decision to the best of your ability, that hard decision — that terribly hard decision, an unusual thing occurs. Suddenly, as though turning the person and looking in a new way, we see the positive things about them — that sweet, cute smile, the way they held us or took care of us. The way they did that wonderful thing that they do, we think on those things. You remember the time you were driving down the street, the top was down, the sun shining, your favorite song was playing, you were in love. He turned, took your hand and said, "Why can't it always be this way?" What a great question.

When you are thinking the wonderful things about that person and wondering, "Why did we separate — why did we cut the ties?" Stop yourself and think about the reasons you did it. Think about the reasons you gave up on the relationship. Realize you made the right decision.

The Position of Strength

Sometimes, we realize we made the wrong decision. What do we do? In a relationship or a friendship, we all want to deal from a position of strength. We don't want to grovel. We don't want to be the needy one, the one begging for forgiveness. Look at Jerry and Marie.

Ribbons That Tie

A friend of mine separated from his wife. She was unfaithful; he was unfaithful. They grew up together, been married for 15 years and have two kids. They love each other. He realizes that he loves her and doesn't want to lose her. At this point, she is pushing him away. What's the right thing to do? The right thing is for him to be kind and caring and to tell her, "Thank you for the most beautiful thing in my life: you, my family and our children."

Jerry needs to tell Marie the truth, the good truth, without giving in to being vindictive. He needs to tell her he loves her, still wants to take care of her, to be parents together to their two children. To be vindictive or hateful burns the bridge and tears the wonderful ribbons that tie them together. If he truly wants to have a chance for their love and relationship to grow, for it to become more than either one imagines, Jerry needs to let her go. Tell her he loves her and let her go. It's hard. It's hard. But, this is the position of strength.

He should not be with her intimately, not be mean to her, not tell her what a terrible mother, mate, etc., she has been. Jerry needs to see that he has been just as much a failure as Marie and welcome compassion into his relationship. Once he gets past the vindictive, the hurting, the torturing and becomes a kind, supportive man, if she is meant to return, if she wants to be with him, she'll come back.

Stay Strong

It can't be in a week or two weeks. He must stay strong. He must not be in a physical relationship. Because, if he gives in too quick, when she breaks down or he breaks down and tells you she wants to come back, be the wife, be the mother, know that the same thing will happen again and again. This is the hardest thing you may ever do. Most people don't have that strength. But if he waits a month or two and the other comes to that point where she sees what she is really losing, and they both realize what they have, they think about the good things, they dwell on the good. They reminisce. They remember the sweet things and realize who you really are and love you anyway. They'll come back.

He Stayed a Friend

Or, if they don't come back, it's not meant to be. You must be strong enough to do this even though, more than anything, you want to be the person with that person. One of the things about relationships with friends or companions, when we end that relationship, some people choose to talk about and emphasize the painful things. The right thing to do is to forgive the awful things, tell them you are not in love but you still love them and you always will and that's the truth. It might be hard. Never burn a bridge! Jerry was strong. He stayed separated. He stayed a friend. He stayed the father of their children. Two months later, they had a date and they restored their marriage, only now, at a new, higher level. They went through the valley, endured the pain and chose to be together again.

When you live in the truth with love in your heart, it will set you both free. Forgive.

That Magic Something

Something magic happens when we release our personal, ego driven desires. Elizabeth and Pete had been married for 30 years. She left him. He wept, begged and pleaded with her to come back. Pete desperately wanted Elizabeth to stay with him. He was devastated.

Then, one night he went with a friend to a party — and, yep, you got it — met a girl. The terrific clutches he had on his mate released. He let go. And, said, "I bet Elizabeth will want to come back now that I've met someone else." He was right. The very next day, Liz called and wanted to come back to the relationship.

The True Friend

The true friend is someone who has a pretty good idea who we are, who sees behind the mask, and loves us anyway. The true friend loves us in spite of our flaws, in spite of our failures, in spite of the times we've lied, haven't listened, pretended, and didn't show up. The true friend loves us through all of our pretense.

When someone shares something personal and deep with you, it's hard not to be judgmental. The true friend stops to think before he reacts or speaks. The true friend knows we've failed. The true friend is one who knows you and loves you anyway.

To Be a True Friend

The True Friend knows we have all failed and yet, chooses to see the good. The true friend chooses to see the beautiful things, to see the cup half full, to see the stars through the bars in every situation. You have a choice. Yes, it's just that simple. To be a true friend means to choose to see the positive, to see the good.

Forgive

Your Power Move

How vital is forgiveness? We all make mistakes. We're mean, we're cruel and we're selfish. We do things we know are wrong. Forgiveness is an incredible part of our lives. If we weren't forgiven, if we didn't forgive, we would be forever condemned, crucified by ourselves and everyone we know. If we weren't forgiven, we'd have no friends, no family, no hope and no love. If we didn't forgive, we'd hate everyone; if they didn't forgive, everyone would hate us. We'd deserve it and they would deserve it.

Please Forgive Me

Please forgive me. I beg for your forgiveness. If I can be forgiven, if you can forgive me, if I can forgive you, we can start over with a clean slate. I feel joy in my heart. I feel redeemed. Yeah, we will mess up again. And I'll ask for your forgiveness. Will you ask for mine?

When we're beyond doubt forgiven, unconditionally, without any strings attached, free and clear, we have true joy.

Right Now!

Why wait? Do it now! Right now! Put Best Day down. Call them. Go see them. Ask for their forgiveness. Keep asking them until they say, "I forgive you." Tell them you're doing your best. Tell them you made a mistake.

I'm a Sinner

I'm not a religiously schooled person, but I am very spiritual. One of the truly beautiful things in the Christian belief is God giving His only Son so that we can be forgiven. He knew we couldn't be perfect or follow all the rules. He didn't want us to carry the burden of all the terrible things we've done because no one would get to Heaven. Forgive yourself.

On Easter I had a party. I said a prayer. I love Easter. I love that we're forgiven. I am sorry I sinned. But, I'm a sinner. It's nice to be forgiven.

Hate Hurts

When somebody hurts you or does something mean or devious, is that something you want to carry around inside you? Is it something you think about when you see that person or that thing, whatever it is that reminds you of that hurtful time?

Think about it. Is it hurting you — the terrible thing they did? Yes. You're carrying around hurt. Have you ever had somebody forgive you? Really forgive you? For something you did that was terribly wrong? When they did this, did you think about what you did? Did you feel worse? Did you apologize? Did you tell them it was wrong? Did you hear them? Even if they forgave you, the only way to true forgiveness is to forgive yourself first. It always starts with you — no, not you, me!

Let's Get Even!

Do you want retribution? Do you want to get even? Do you want to hurt them back? Do you want revenge to make them pay? Do you want them to admit their wrong? Do you know they don't deserve your forgiveness?

Forgive Them

We have all done something that's so bad we've never even shared that something with anybody else. Fix it. Apologize. Sincerely, tell the truth. We're all sinners. We all fail. We're all just doing our best. But yes, we can do better. We've all done terrible things in our lives. Forgive yourself.

The ATM Heist

I'll tell you a story about one of my best friends. I still see him three times a week. I love him; he loves me. He is a building contractor and volunteered to build a shed for me. I gave him my ATM card and told him to buy whatever supplies he needed. When he was done with the job, I forgot about my card. About four months later, I went to the ATM to get some money; the machine said I had taken out my limit for that day. I hadn't left my house in two days, so I called the bank to see what was up.

I got all the records. My friend had been using my card, taking out small sums at first, gradually increasing to a total of $8,400. He justified the action by telling himself he was going to pay me back; he actually kept a record!

Hurt Back or Forgive

I thought about it for a day or two. I pictured him taking the money out. I considered calling the police. I wanted revenge. I thought about retribution. I was hurt and I wanted to hurt back. I wanted to get even!

Then I remembered the bad stuff I had done in my life. I mess up all the time. I've lied, I've stolen, etc., etc., etc. I called him up and told him I loved him. I told him to come over we needed to talk. We talked. We cried. I forgave him. He paid me back every penny in less than a month.

In His Own Eyes

After, when I saw him, there was no smile, no joy in his eyes. He didn't want to be around our friends. Of course, he longed to be with us because we're best friends but he'd done such a terrible thing in his own eyes, he couldn't forgive himself.

I sat down with him and told him, "Buddy, we all make mistakes. We all do things that are terrible. We're human. Forgive yourself. I forgive you. I'll never talk about it again. I love you. I know you love me. Let it go. Get rid of it. I can forgive you but, unless you forgive yourself, you'll never be healed. You'll carry it around forever."

Run on Water

Some of my friends didn't understand this. They thought I was stupid. They said, "How could you ever trust him? How can you even trust him in your home? Why would you want to be friends with someone who did this to you?"

"You know why? I didn't want to carry it around. I didn't want to feel bad about it."

Now, our friendship's stronger than ever. I'd trust him with anything. He'd walk on water for me. I'd run on water for him. It's easy to talk about it. It's easy to know the right thing to do. Do it. Forgive and then, forgive some more. Fix the things you haven't fixed. Right the wrongs that you can. If the person's gone or it's something you can't fix with them because they're passed away or whatever reason, it's time to forgive yourself. Love yourself. Love others. Is it really just that simple?

Can I just forgive them? Will they really forgive me? If you say it and mean it, if you make sure they hear you or you hear them, it will change your life. It will change their life. You'll be better. They'll be better. Fix it. Fix it now. It's up to you. You must forgive yourself, first. It's harder to forgive yourself than to forgive someone else.

After you forgive yourself, they will forgive you. Yeah, I make it sound easy. Is it really just that easy? Be mentally tough. Smile. Fix it. Fix it now.

How?

Realize that we're all bad. We all make mistakes. We all miss the mark. Forgive yourself unconditionally. How do I forgive myself unconditionally? Once again, realize we all make mistakes — how about that term 'I'm only human'? There's no good without bad, no black without white. Let it go. Dwell on the good. Realize you're going to make mistakes. You can do better. We can all do better. Forgive. You may not forget. Learn from it. Don't do it again. But, hey, we're only human and we're all forgiven if we, in turn, forgive.

Change Your Life

It will change your life; it will change their life. It's up to you. Don't start today. Start now. See the beauty. See the love. It's just that simple. If you insist on dwelling on the negative, the bad, it's your fault, it's your choice. Dwell on the good. Dwell on how you ask for forgiveness. Dwell on the fact that you knew you were wrong, you knew you lied, you knew you were bad. I asked for forgiveness. I was forgiven.

I forgive myself. Learn from your mistakes. We all make them, every day. We're just doing our best. I'm going to do a whole lot better. Start now. Start this very moment. We forgive you. I forgive you. Forgive yourself. Ask for forgiveness — you shall be forgiven. "Oh that's ridiculous. It can't be that easy."

You shallow negative person.

15

Success

Enjoy your lifetime

What is success? Those people are flooded with success; they have that beautiful house, two Mercedes, so much material wealth. Does that mean they are successful? Maybe. Maybe not. During our sales seminars, I use an analogy: If you work 60 hours a week, have a Porsche, a Mercedes and a swimming pool, does that make you successful? No. Success is to enjoy each and every moment — not day or week — in your life. Success is to be happy now — and now — and now.

A Friend Named Boo

I have a friend named Boo. Boo went to the beach every day. He'd play volleyball, have fun with his dog, swim in the ocean, Frisbee, golf, watch the sunset, sing, and play, play, play. His girlfriend was a bartender at the best bar in town — free drinks, free food. *She* took *him* on vacation.

Boo and Michael Ann married. Now, he works five days a week and has a beautiful family. His wife's family is very wealthy and I would often tease him, "You're the richest man I know, Boo." And Boo quickly defended himself saying, "We don't own any of that money yet."

"Boo, I'm not talking about the money. I'm talking about your sons David and Quinn and your beautiful wife Michael Ann (yes, she was the bar tender), her perfect smile. And what about your home in Bonny Doon, your garden, the deck you built from the redwoods you milled from your own trees (and to this day, he shows it to me every time I go to his house): these make you the richest man I know.

"When you talk about your children, your big beautiful eyes fill with tears. That's success. It has nothing to do with the money you have or the money you might get in the future." *

Save It For the Kids

In my job, by the way, I quit two weeks ago to write this book for you and me and the world, every day, I meet many people, most over 65. Some were living their dreams, spending the money they worked so hard for. But, many of them had four million dollars in the bank, owned their own home, wore tennis shoes from Walmart and the same polyester pants every time I saw them. They dreamed about owning a motor home, going out and seeing the United States. They'd come in, year after year, to pick out their dream coach. But they never get their dream coach, never see the United States because they saved their money. They died with four million dollars in the bank and a home that was paid for.

"I'm saving it for our kids." I heard that a lot. This is so, so sad. They fell into a hoarding mode. They didn't allow themselves to spend any of it. They drive the same old Taurus, they live in the same house in the middle of industrial San Jose and never let themselves live their dreams.

Live Your Life

Were they successful? I don't know. I just know they should have spent all their money. Isn't that the purpose of work?

Live your lives. Live your dreams. Don't wait until tomorrow. Start today. Start now. The reason I work so hard is not because I want others to say, "Look, he's so successful." It's because I like to swim in my pool, drive my car with the top down, go to dinner and buy a nice bottle of wine. I want to go on vacation, lay on the beach. I don't care about *being* rich; I enjoy the things money helps me buy.

Success is —

Success is to enjoy yourself. Success is to be a good person, a good friend. Success is to feel good about yourself. Success is to be happy. Success is to love and to be loved. Success is to be friends with your parents and your friends. Success is to enjoy every moment of every day.

Ceeks

I have many friends who believe they are not successful. My friend Ceeks seems so successful. His girl friend Louise wants him to be rich. When she says "rich", she's talking about material wealth — you know — get a real job. He struggles with this. He lives in Maui, works at the beach, taking pictures of tourists. He has so much talent. He could do anything he wants: a salesman, go to Hollywood, be an actor or a comedian.

I sat him down and talked to him. "Charles Johnson (serious talk), look at where you live, look at what you do. We swam with the whales today. You touched one. The dolphins almost jumped in the boat. We barbecued. We played Frisbee. We had conversations with Chris Berman and Tommy Thayer. I played volleyball with Grant Windstrom (by the way, he was defensive player of the year in the NFL). They were famous people. These people try to find you, know you by name, Ceeks, because you are so funny, you're so happy, you radiate joy and love."

Ceeks had big tears in his eyes when he told me this story.

Ceeks's Story

"When I was a child, my mother left us. We lived with my dad who was a traveling salesman. I was 10. We had no running water. I had to steal water to bathe my brother and me. My father re-married. He was never there. She had her own children. She cut my fingernails so short so that if I touched something, my fingers would bleed and she would know. When we came home from school, she locked me in the shed. She'd hit me. She'd torture me. Then she left and he remarried."

Ceeks's father was dying when he told this story and he poured his heart out.

"Everybody believes I am this happy, funny, cool guy."

"Ceeks, you are. Look at what you've overcome! Look at who you've become. Let's go look in the mirror together. That person, those people think you are, that's who you are. You're beautiful. You're kind. You're honest.

"Ceeks, can you forgive your father, your mother, your step-mother? Can you forgive them, Ceeks? You've been carrying this around your whole life."

Ceeks said, "I don't think so."

"Think about the terrible things, the awful things you've done in your life. Can you forgive yourself? Let it go?"

The next time I talked to Ceeks, he had talked to his stepmother, made up with her; his father had passed away, but his father knew Ceeks loved him and Ceeks knew his father loved him.

Ceeks is one of the most successful people I know. No money. No stuff. Goes to the beach, watches the sunset. Should he move to Hollywood and become a big star? He'd have to live in Los Angeles. Ceeks smiles. He sees the truth in these words. Do you?

Enemy Hurt Hurts You

Success is to be happy now. Success is to forgive yourself now. Success is to forgive people who are our enemies. We carry that enemy hurt deep in our hearts. We justify having enemies, being mean to people because of the things they have done. Even if it is our fault, we make up a story to make it their fault. Don't even bother to carry it around. It hurts us. Start being successful today. Know how free you are to choose. You are, you know! Be happy now. We have a choice. We have a certain amount of time that we spend on this earth. We have a choice to be happy or to be miserable, to be mean or to be nice, to make friends or to make enemies. Chose to be happy. Choose to love. Choose to find the good in everything.

Half Full or Overflowing?

I'm not saying you shouldn't go to work. I'm not saying you don't need money. I'm just saying when you do go to that job, you have a choice to be happy or unhappy. I have a choice to be happy or bummed out. You have a choice to be happy or bummed. Be happy no matter where you live or what you do. You have a choice. I have a choice. We are free to choose. It's just that simple.

Leave a Success Trail

We all make mistakes. We're all just doing our best. We all have bad days. ***Choose to focus on the good things in a bad situation.*** Choose to be successful. Choose to be happy. Find the good in everything. You can do it. It's just that simple. Choose to help the people around you be successful. Choose to help them see the good in everything. Choose to be positive. Choose to listen. Choose to help. Choose to make the world successful, not just yourself, but everywhere you go, leave a success trail behind you. ***Envision a success trail ahead of you.*** Success behind and ahead. Happy Trails To You!

** My dear friend Boo was killed in an automobile accident. He was 45. At his memorial service, 25 persons went to the podium and each fervently said, "Boo was my best friend." That is the kind of man we can all strive to be. I named our little girl after you, Boo. Bazil Boo.*

Miss You, Boo

16

Work

Dark chocolate Milky Ways

Work, is that a swear word? I don't think so. How do you define work? When I think of work, I think of doing something I don't really enjoy. Yet, work is an essential part of our day-to-day existence. Work is the way we provide for our family, our friends and ourselves. It is what most of us do five days a week, 40 hours a week. Some of us gripe about going to work. Some of us like to work.

The Job

Is work where we go, put in our time and then get paid a certain amount of money for our efforts? This defines "work" in a term that we all recognize but don't appreciate. I think we should have more words for work. Let's make some.

Is This Work?

Is it still work when we love to do it? I am *working* on my volley ball game. I'm *working* on being a better hugger. I'm *working* on my tan. I'm *working* on the exact ingredients for that perfect margarita. I'm *working* on my book. I'm *working* on my relationships with my parents, wife, friends, loved ones and not so loved ones. I'm *working* with my dog. I'm *working* on making that perfect cup of coffee.

If I got paid for these things, would that make it work? Would it?

I Hate My Job

Do you enjoy your job? Do you dwell on the idea that it's not fun and you don't like being there?

"I hate my job, but I have to go to work to support my family, myself, pay the rent, pay the credit card and survive. Even if we hate our job, we still get joy out of it."

"How can you say that?"

"It was a great steak. It was a great salad. I'm putting my kids through college. I love my home. I bought the most beautiful flowers today. I love my new car. I love my horse. I love to eat. I hate my job. Am I willing to put in eight hours a day at a job that I hate to support myself and my family? The answer is a resounding 'YES'.

"Not only 'YES' but, when I think of all the blessings my friends and my family receive through my job, I like it a lot better after all. I appreciate having a job that allows me all these privileges and pleasures! I enjoy the things my work supplies."

I Love My Job

How many people do you know who like to work? If you hate your work, you are probably in the wrong job. If I got paid to work on my tan, would I still enjoy it? Yes. I'm working right now — writing this for you. I'm making the world and myself better. It brings great joy to me. My Mom was a great counselor. She taught parenting and active listening. She taught people how to be better people. She loves her job. She's helping people and families. She's making the world a better place. She loves to help people. She loves to love people. "My job *is* loving," she told me "Love takes the pain out of work — out of life."

If you have to be there, enjoy, what do you have to lose?

Bring flowers to work. Bring a cake. Smile and say "Good morning" and "Hello" to everyone, from the guy who cleans the bathrooms to the person who runs the business. It might not be your favorite part of the day or the week but, if you have to be there, be happy. **Choose to be happy. What do you have to lose?**

You Looked so Happy

Mom says, "I thought you loved your job. You always looked so happy."

"Here's my secret. Every day when I went to work, I smiled and said hello to everybody. My office was a sanctuary of positive healing advice, good, sound advice. If you walked into my office 365 days a year, 360 of those days, I would smile, tell a joke say, 'Let's go to work and make some money.'

Adam at Work

"I'd have the right answers, listen and be supportive. I always closed my meetings with, 'Have fun and make a lot of money!'" Do you think they miss me?

Eating Cheese

The hardest part of my job was interpersonal relationships with the people who worked there. I was the Father of the family — a dysfunctional family. I would routinely apologize to somebody when I did absolutely nothing wrong. "Whatever I did to hurt you or make you feel bad, I apologize." I call this 'eating cheese'. Why would I apologize to somebody when I did nothing wrong? If I didn't, I'd have to deal with it on an everyday basis: no hello, no good morning, no hugs, no smiles. I learned to *manage my environment* so that people around me and myself could be happy.

Mikie and Milky Ways

I had a salesman named Mike. I took Mike's job when I was hired nine years ago. Mike is a volatile guy. He's a beautiful warm, cuddly bear, but he would completely lose it and scream and yell at anybody close enough for him to attack once every three months. When we first started, I'd yell back and tell him why he was wrong. He would get me to fight with him so he could dump his anger on me. We would fight and yell. He would leave work. It would last a long time.

I learned to let Mikie yell — no matter how hurtful, no matter how long. Mikie loved dark, chocolate Milky Ways. When he was done, I bought him a candy bar. I wouldn't fight with him, I wouldn't yell, I wouldn't let him affect me in a negative way. I wouldn't let the terrible things he said hurt me. He needed to scream and yell to release something inside of him. After I gave him the candy bar, three to five minutes later, he apologized to everyone, gave me a hug and said, "I'm sorry. Thank you, Adam."

I miss that part of my job.

Be the Best

We don't all have these options, but we can be the best. If you're digging a ditch, dig a beautiful ditch; if you're a gardener, make a beautiful garden; if you're a sales person, be the best sales person; if you're a writer, be the best writer. I'm not saying you'll be the best salesperson, the best writer *in the world* — be the best digger, the best salesperson, the best writer *you* can be.

If you love your job, you're lucky and you're blessed. If you don't, try to make it better before you quit because, more than likely, you're not going to like your next job either.

When We're Grown

Most of us don't choose what we're going to do when we're grown and, even if we do make a choice, many times, it is not truly the work we were destined to do. The best thing to do is to make the best of your situation now, realizing that work is a necessity. Don't resent your work, appreciate and value your work. You will transform your self, your job and others in your workplace. Remember, there's no play without work; there's no good without bad. It's the nature of life. You might as well enjoy yourself. What have you got to lose? It's just that simple.

Your Perfect Job

What is your perfect job? My perfect job would be to be a trust fund guy. If you had millions and millions, would you still work? Most persons say they would. They wouldn't do something they didn't enjoy. They might coach, they might teach and they might be fishermen. And, guess what? They'd still have bad days and challenges: the team lost their games; the kids wouldn't listen; they didn't catch any fish and the boat broke down.

It's Never What We Picture

Even if we choose our own perfect job, it's still hard. It won't be what we pictured. Isn't this the nature of everything in life? We have a choice. I'll fix my boat. I'll find the fish. I learned a lot coaching this season; I'm going to be a much better coach. I want to win. I want to be successful at my occupation. Would success be to win all 11 games? Or, would success be to take the worst player on my team who didn't get to play much but loved to be there and let him know he is part of the team? Or, should we quit again? That's the easy way out. We're probably in the situation we're in because it was the best job we could find. Or, we might be there because we have more to learn. What do you think?

Make Them Better

Bosses generally want to take credit for all the good at your work. Can you help him/her be a better boss without taking credit for it? If you want your work situation to improve, help the boss; in turn, you'll be helping yourself.

Be smart. Help them in a way that let's them take credit for it. Tell them they are good bosses, encourage them, give them your ideas, and help them think it is their idea. Of course, you know the truth.

Are You Your Problem?

Are YOU the problem at your job? Do you blame others for your shortcomings? Can you do better at your job? We can all do better. After you write down the good and the bad, how much of the bad are you responsible for? How much of the good are you responsible for? What can you change to make it better?

These questions require answers and choices only you can make. Do you have an abusive/mean boss — or a demanding boss? Do you like your boss? Do you dislike your boss? Are you a good boss? Can you be a better boss? Can you fix the relationship? Can you communicate with your boss/owner?

"I Quit"

"I quit. I'll get a new job." Quitting is a huge decision. Before you take that step, be sure it is the right one. Talk to your friends about it. Get feedback. Talk to the people who work at the new place. Make sure you know what you're getting paid; that's why you're going to work. If you must support yourself and/or your family, never quit unless you have a new job. The only time this is an option is when we're working on a month-to-month basis to pay our bills and we have another job set up — another job we perceive to be better, one we like more, that will produce enough income to pay our bills and support our lifestyle.

Before you quit, sit down, think about the good things and the bad things about your job. What's going to be better wherever you are going? Is it truly going to be better?

Keep Your Focus

Is there a person at your work place who is happy? Who's successful? Success is to enjoy every moment, remember that. There are also those individuals who gossip, complain, criticize, or disrupt the ebb and flow of our day-to-day work.

Example: There were 14 salespeople. We came to work, went to breakfast, read the paper, talked about sports and we barbecued. Some sat out on the sales floor and talked about how slow it was, how hot it was and how they got cheated out of money. They focused upon and magnified the negative even though the worst salesman at our dealership made over $120,000 a year; the best made around $300,000. They could still find something to criticize, to complain about. Don't be one of those complainers. Don't give them your energy. When they say something negative, don't buy into it. Let it pass and keep *your* focus.

Ten Cents An Hour

There are those who work for 10 cents an hour, working 12, 14, 16 hours a day. They work in factories and farms. Some of them enjoy their jobs. Some of them are thankful to have a job. We are so blessed to be workers in the USA. We're so lucky to have our jobs. Those people have a choice to enjoy their jobs or to sit around and dwell on the negative. If they could get a better job, they wouldn't be working here for the last 10 years. So, why not enjoy the good things about the job. The fact that we don't have to dig ditches or fight wars might be comparison enough for each one of us to be grateful. If we look and see the good in whatever environment we are in, there's always good there if we choose to see it. *The good always outweighs the bad.*

The point I am getting across is: if we're going to be there for 40, 50, or 60 hours a week, see the good in it. See the beautiful things on a day-to-day basis. Choose to see the good. It's up to you. It's that simple. Choose the good. What have you got to lose by being happy?

Enjoy each and every day of your life. Be the best ditch digger you can. There is pride in all jobs. There is good in all work. If you're a carpenter and you hate to go to work, when the house you built is completed, do you still feel a sense of pride in your work? Do you feel good about what you created? That's the part we must see on a day-to-day basis. Find the good. Choose the good. Love what you're doing.

My Pop, "A Worker Guy"

Some people say when we stop working, we start dying. My Pop has plenty of money to retire. I tell him, "Why don't you guys quit working, go on vacation and spend your money?" In his case, work is what he does. Work is who he is. He's been financially successful in his endeavors. He was a penniless son of sharecroppers. When

he was nine, his mother died. His father only knew how to make biscuits and gravy. My Pop got sick and they took him to the County hospital where he stayed, without mother or father in the hospital for 12 months.

He retired once when he was 40. He went back to college and got a degree in history and religion. When he was done, he started in business again. He feels good about himself when he works. He feels successful. Work makes him happy. He comes alive when he is working on a project. He tells Mom, "Let's build a new house." He loves to make money for his family. He is the great provider. He is a great role model. He is a great worker.

Maria Times — Thursday, March 8, 2001

Business Roundup

Best Storage owner eyes Betteravia site

John A. Read
Times Business Editor

Elmer Garrison, who built **Best Storage** on Santa Maria Way and later purchased the ministorage units in the Skyway Drive complex, isn't through providing small spaces for the world.

The Avila Beach-based builder is contemplating a suite of industrial shop spaces along the south side of Betteravia Road west of the Blosser-Skyway intersection. It will probably be a year before he gets plans through the process, and he isn't sure at the moment how many units there will be, but 20 could work, he said.

The structure would have a decorative rock wall along the front and block wall spaces behind.

Garrison's Santa Maria Way facility got a close look from the Atascadero Planning Department when Garrison went before that agency for a ministorage complex in North County.

"They said, 'We want one like that,' " Garrison said. They got one, 293 units worth, slightly less than the 323 here. The units are popular, with an occupancy rate of about 95 percent due to transients, he said.

Vacation/Work? —
It's All the Same

He doesn't want to go on vacation. He wants to go to work. It is who he is. It's what makes him feel good about himself. He is really good at what he does. He glows when he works. In the work situation, he always knows what to say, he always knows what to do — and he loves doing it. Is it still work? I don't think so. It's like me working on my tan, mixing that perfect margarita, working on my volleyball game. No, that's not quite right. It's like me working on this book. It's something I do for myself, for my friends, for everybody in the world to make the world a better place, to make my friends happier, to give my children something when I pass away.

The Right Work Brings Goodness

We need more definitions for work because, in this case, it's life. It's our love. It's me giving something to the world, making things better for my friends. It's me leaving a legacy for my daughter Bazil Boo. I feel good about myself. I'm doing the right thing. The right thing brings goodness.

So, What is Work?

We're still trying to define work. It is many things. Let's try it again.

Work: a task I perform to support myself and my family
Work: something I love and totally enjoy doing
Work: efforts to help others — peace corp, save whales, etc.
Work: trying to make the world a better place
Work: because I love to work

Work has many meanings — many good jobs and many bad jobs. But, one thing we know, we all must work. It is a huge part of who we are. After writing this, I'm feeling a lot better about my job. I guess I liked it better than I thought.

I Quit So You Could Read This Book

I quit so you could read this book. I remember calling Mom, being really upset, telling her, "Mom, I want to write this book. The words keep coming to me. I need to quit my job, but I just can't bring myself to do it."

There was a time to quit. It was the right decision for me.

Never Burn a Bridge

When I left, this is the letter I wrote:

ADAM GOLDBERG
APTOS, CALIFORNIA

July 11, 2005

To: Team Promise RV

What a wonderful ride!
Thanks for the opportunity to work with you.
Thanks for your constant support.
Thanks for your guidance. Thanks for being great friends.
Thanks for being great co-workers. Thanks for being great boss-es, great counselors, great owners.
It has been a true privilege to work with the best, the very best.
You helped my family. You helped me grow as a person, a friend and a manager. I can't thank each one of you enough.

       Love,
        Adam

Never burn a bridge. Life is what *you* make of it. Wherever you are, have fun, smile. It's the first thing people notice about you. Design a vision for your purpose in life. Be happy. It's just that simple. How's your day?

17

Attitude

Is attitude everything?

Is attitude important? Is attitude everything? It's not everything but it's close. When I'm asked, "How are you doing?" I say, "This is my best day ever and, tomorrow, tomorrow is going to be a little better." This is the truth for me. You can make it the truth for you. Dwell on the good. See the beauty. See the stars through the bars. Is your half full cup half empty or half full? Yours is overflowing. Mine is overflowing. It's just that simple. A positive mental attitude is up to you. What do you choose?

Mental Toughness

An affirmative attitude can be yours; you need mental toughness and a determined focus. We all have bad days. Even in a bad day, there's *so much more good than bad.* Focus on the good. Stay strong. Smile. It's the first thing people notice about you. Yours is a beautiful smile. Remember? Make friends. Be nice. Stay strong. Love yourself. Love your friends. Love your enemies. Don't hate them. That hurts you and your enemies.

"How can I love my enemies?" you ask. Why are they your enemies? It's probably just as much your fault as theirs. Forgive them. You're thinking, "They are the ones who should be forgiving me!" Beat them to the punch. You forgive them. You'll reap your reward.

We know people who always seem happy, who smile, who are positive, who have a great attitude. It's simple. It's mental toughness. You have a choice. Choose to see the good, the hopeful, the wonderful. It's that simple.

There are mean people, angry people and negative people. We're those people. Get over it. Take responsibility. Stop blaming your childhood and your parents. Stop blaming your spouse. Stop blaming yourself. Stop punishing yourself. Stop punishing the people around you. Forgive them. Forgive yourself. It all starts with you. No, not you, me. Do better. Be that person you want to be. Be strong. Be loving. Make friends wherever you go.

Be Thankful

Be thankful for what you have. It doesn't have to be to give thanks to God; it can be whoever it is that you talk to. That Something you talk to when we swell with joy and speak to the wonder of it all, when we see the beautiful sunrise, that gorgeous sunset, our child's first smile. Rejoice in life. Hey, this is not a dress rehearsal. We're not at practice. This is life. Choose to be strong. Choose to be just. Choose to be thankful. Choose to be honest. It's just that simple.

Choose to love. Choose to forgive. Choose to forgive yourself first. Forgive everyone. We all do bad things. See the good in yourself. See the good in others. Connect with the positive.

Be The Beauty. Be The Good.

Bad things happen to us. You can't escape that. There's no life without death. There's no black without white. There's no love without hate. There's no good without bad. You're dying of cancer. Even if you've been given that death sentence, and we all have because life and death are one and the same, be happy. Dwell on the good things of life: the love, the sunset, the sunrises, that special smile, a good book. Never stop learning. You might as well be happy. What have you got to lose?

Never stop loving. Never stop living. Never stop trying to be a better person. No, that's wrong. Don't try to be a better person; be a better person. Don't try to be happy, be happy. Don't try to love more, love more. See the beauty. See the good. Be the beauty. Be the good.

Attitude is mental toughness, seeing the good. Attitude loves. Attitude is up to you. Let's be happier. Let's be more loving. Let's be more forgiving. I love you. Your friends love you. Your family loves you. Dwell on love. Be thankful for the freedom you have to choose. Change your attitude today. Change your attitude now. It really is just that simple.

Now is the Living Moment

How's your day? It's my Best Day Ever. I'm thinking, "Tomorrow will be a little better." This is not a wishful thought, an idle statement; this is our reality. Yes it's hard. It's up to us and it's just that simple. If we choose to be happy, loving, honest, successful, a role model for the world, then, that's who we will be! Be mentally tough. Today is all we have. Now is the living moment. Tomorrow will be a little better, even though, this is my best day yet.

18

Happiness Now

See the stars through the bars

Most know people who seem to be always happy, always up — always positive. They smile. They talk about interesting things in the paper. They talk about the sports page. They talk about what they are going to do. They say, "It's going to be sunny tomorrow." They show you a funny or happy cartoon. They are up, happy, joyful and want to share that with you.

And, we know people who tell you about the flesh-eating disease, the terrible floods, the earthquakes, the murders and the awful things that happen. Ninety percent of their conversation dwells on the negative. They don't smile. They don't laugh. They carry the pains of the world on their backs, on their frowns, and maybe, in their hearts. Guess what? They are delighted to pass this on to you!

These folks have turned their life focus onto pessimistic ways of thinking. They might be surrounded with much beauty but they have chosen to look at the dark side. Why?

What's the difference between these two people? Was it the way they were raised, the way they were parented? Do they blame their negative view on their upbringing? On their job, their boss, their "day", their husbands or their wives? Where they live? Their surroundings? Their neighbors? They usually blame it on somebody or something other than themselves.

Happiness Now!

At some point in time, take responsibility for the way you think — what you think about, your focus. "The day is dumb — the day is a wonderful opportunity." It's all up to you. By the way, that time is now! You can be a happy person. It all depends on the way you think.

You have a beautiful smile. Remember? It's the first thing people notice about you. There is no yesterday. Yesterday is gone. Will there be a tomorrow? Well, I sure hope so. How's your day? Best Day Ever? I'm thinking, tomorrow might be a little better. You can be happy. You can choose to see the good in life. I can be happy. I can choose to see the good all around me.

Yeah, I know there are terrible things going on in the world. Acknowledge them. Yes. Acknowledge the bad things. Talk about them if it's something you can fix. We can't fix everything. Fix what you can. Help the world. Save the whales. Do what you can.

Which to Think About

When you think about the whales, do you think about the whaling boats out there killing them — the blood in the water?

Have you ever been in the water with the whales? Ever watch them play? See them leap out of the water, heaving their massive beauty? When you are in the water, you can hear them talk. They're majestic. They're beautiful. They're special.

See the good. See the positive on a day-to-day basis. You have a choice every second — every day of your life to be happy, to see the beauty, to love and to care. Think about the whales, smile that they are no longer almost extinct. They're spectacular. They're coming back. Sure, somebody's killing them some place and that's terrible. But, I have a choice. I have a choice which one to think about. Guess what genius? So do you!

Never Let an Asshole Ruin Your Day!

Every day of your life, someone will try to ruin your day. You can count on it. You don't have to let them. "That son of a bitch just cut me off." Wave at them. Smile. Guess what? They will probably shake their head and smile too. Never let an asshole ruin your day. Don't buy into it. Forgive him. Feel sorry for him. Sorry about the *asshole.* (Mom cringes when she writes my swear words.) It gets the point across.

Wherever you are, whatever you're doing, you have a choice. You have a choice to be happy or gloomy. You have a choice to see the bad or the good. It's up to you. Do you want to smile? Do you want to frown? Do you want to laugh?

Our Thoughts Power Us — Up or Down

"But, I don't want to be nice to that person. But, they're mean. But, they lied. But, they cut me off. But, they hunt whales." But, But, But, But — that must be our worst word! It is reassuring to justify the way we feel — even if it sinks us deeper into a negative hole. We want to make it true by the way we think. Guess what? We do???

See the Stars

Let's say you are put in jail. You can't get out. What do you do? You're thinking, "How can I be happy in this situation?" Couldn't you be happy just as easy as you could be sad? What benefit do you get out of feeling crummy? When you look out of the window of your cell, what do you see? Do you see the bars? Right past the bars are beautiful stars. Do you see the bars or the stars? No matter how bad things are, you still have a choice. Find a sunny spot where the sun shines through the window. Feel the warm sun on your face. Read a book. Study something you love.

Look up. See the stars through the bars. ***Find the good — find the good. In everything you have a choice.*** If you're locked in jail, should you dwell on the bad? Why you're there? What good is that for you?

No matter where you are, there's good people and bad people. Dwell on the good. What's the good in jail? Three decent meals a day, a dry place to sleep, opportunity to learn, opportunity to study — lots of time. Almost everybody I know who's been in jail comes out looking like Arnold Swartznager. You have a choice. You can choose to be happy. Does this sound ridiculous to you that somebody could be in jail and be happy and successful?

A Problem? Learning Opportunity

When you leave the house today, take this one day and do this. Say "Hello". When they say hello back, listen and smile. If somebody comes to you with a problem, help him or her. A problem is a great learning opportunity. See the positive. Help others. Don't flip off the driver — wave. Say, "Nice car."

"I'm mad." Why? Why not fix it? Why not find some good in it. Why not find the positive person in you? That's really you? What are you hiding???

Mental Toughness

It takes mental toughness. Mental toughness, mental toughness, mental toughness! Take control of your mind's focus. It's up to you. Yesterday's gone. Why not be happy? Why not be positive? How does being grumpy, disgusted or critical help you? What does that do for you? Or, any one else? Or, for the world? Does this world really need your pain dumped on it? Think about it.

The Greeting

When your loved ones come into your presence, look them in the eye, give them a hug and tell them you love them. This will open that loving path.

The Choice is Yours

No one else can be happy for you. No one else can be positive for you. It's up to you. You have the choice. Is it really just this simple? Can I really just **be happy**? After you've given all those reasons why everything's so bad: read the news, watch TV, my house is a dump, the car doesn't run, my husband's a jerk, my kids don't love me. You've got a place to live. You've got a car — it will run again. Call your kids; ask them to forgive you. Forgive them. Do you love them? Of course you do. Let them know. Give them a hug. **Make** them hug you back. And, when you tell them you love them, make them listen.

Sit down with your husband or wife. Tell the beloved you love him or her. Tell them it's your fault — whatever it was (I know. It's his/her fault!) Forgive. Ask the other to forgive you.

You're Rich!

"I love you." We tell others. We use the term often. You know those times when you really meant it? And you told them? And they didn't hear you? They were trying to find the game? Remember the time you told them, you were holding their face, you were looking at them? They were looking at you? Do it now. Make it better now. Be thankful for what you do have. Realize how blessed you are. Do you know that if you have a dish someplace in your house with coins in it, you're richer than ninety percent of the world? No, that's not the right term. You're not richer, you have more money.

Ten Good Things

You're blessed. You're alive. You bought my book. This means you've got enough money to spend on something besides food and clothing. You're lucky. Can you sit down right now and write ten things that are good, that are happy in your life — about who you are? About the day-to-day world that you live in? Of course, you can. You can write ten bad things, too! Some of them can't be changed. Some of them we have no control over. Stop dwelling on the ten bad things. Learn from them. Dwell on the ten good things. Fix the bad things you can fix. Once again, there is good and bad in everything. Think about the good things.

You!

You have a choice in whatever situation you're in to be happy or dejected. Yes, that's right, *YOU* have a choice. *I* have a choice. *THEY* have a choice. Even if they choose to dwell on the bad, you don't have to. We are free to choose. You have a choice.

Environmental Pollutants

"I'm a happy person, but my mate, parents, boss, whoever it is, dwells on the bad stuff, always polluting my environment." This is a hard situation. Talk to them. I mean, really talk to them. Tell them you need ten minutes of their time because you really want them to hear you, because you care about them and you need them to hear you. If you say, "Hey, you're always negative. Can't you talk about something positive or good?" They'll feel insulted or criticized.

Try this:

Sit down before you talk to them. Think about it. Start by telling them the good things about them. Sometimes it's hard to find the good things. Write them down. There's a reason you're together. "You're a wonderful kisser — you work so hard — you're a wonderful mother or father — you're fun — you're honest — you've got ten fingers and ten toes, etc. etc. etc. I appreciate you." Disarm their defenses to some degree.

Don't Say "You," Say "We"

When you tell them, don't say, "*You* can be more positive." Say, "*We* can be more positive." I know, it's all them. There's two sides to every argument. They're wrong. I'm right. No, you're both wrong; you're both right. You can both do better.

"I'm Not Like That"

When they say, "I'm not like that. It's just the way you perceive me." (Good defense!) Don't get into an argument. Apologize. Tell them you're going to do better. Kill them with kindness. Tell them, "I can do better." Nobody needs to be blamed. You can do better; they can do better; we can do better; I can do better.

"Did You Hear About — ?"

Have you noticed that TV news is almost always negative: disasters, misfortunes, cheating, robberies? The biggest problem in some relationships is the tendency to talk about negative stuff. Sometimes families build their bond through talking about what so and so did — gossiping. "Did you know that he's cheating on her? Can you believe what she did?"

"Try To Do It"

Once, when Patricia was sharing negative news, Dan jumped on the bandwagon. Anything she talked about that was bad, he agreed, he elaborated. Dan told her it was worse than that. Tricia got the message and she started crying and confessed she was just a negative person. She attributed it to her upbringing. "When are you going to start taking responsibility for your day-to-day life?" She replied, "I'm trying."

Don't Try, Do It

Dan said, "Honey, I'm going to *try* to walk through the door." He stubbed his toe, tripped over the dog, fell on the table, broke the vase and slipped on a wet spot. He told her again, "I'm going to walk through the door." And he walked through the door.

"I Need a Hug"

Is it really that simple? Can I just smile instead of frown? "Damn! I'm almost out of wine. Honey, thank you for the half glass of wine. It's fabulous!" It's your perspective on life. It's our perspective on everything. It's attitude. It's a smile. It's a hug. Don't be afraid to say, "I need a hug." Let your partner know she/he is important to you.

Learn From the Bad

Tomorrow's going to be a little better. I'm going to be sweet in the morning. Sorry about my friends, Honey. I'm doing my best. I can do better. Choose the good. See the good. Learn from the bad. Smile. It's the first thing people notice about you.

19

Bring something to the party

A really good hug

(G iving. What an incredible gift. When you give, do you expect something in return? If you do, you'll be disappointed. If you can give unconditionally, you're special.

Bring Something to the Party

True givers bring something to the party. They play with the kids, they smile, they wash dishes, they bring goodies, they cook, they love, they help. We appreciate them.

It's so much more rewarding to be a giver than a taker. I've had friendships with people I thought were great. The more time I spent with them the less I enjoyed their company. They were takers. You know who you are.

You're bitter. You're weary. You don't smile enough. You don't hug your friends. You shake their hands and keep them out of your space. You get the check when you're at dinner, collect the money, tell everybody you need a little more as there's not enough for the tip. You tipped five percent and kept the balance! *They brought nothing to the party.* There are few people in my circle that don't bring something to the party. We don't invite them back!

Giving to Charities

When you give to a charity, are you expecting to get some sort of return? When we give to charities, I think we all hope to receive some benefit. Save the whales. Buy the pastor a new Mercedes. Maybe that will help me be more *in* with God. It seems funny when I write that but, in some churches, give your ten percent and go to heaven!

Ever give to a charity or a cause and discover that ten percent went to the cause? Ouch! Ever give money to a beggar? The ones I can't resist, "Could you give me a few bucks? I need a beer."

There was a lady with her children at McDonalds, counting pennies out for food. Ed bought them all food, ate with them then, played outside with the kids. They had a great time. When she left, Ed gave them all a hug and gave her a 100 bucks. My kind of charity — yours, too?

I Don't Want It!

Each of us has given something to somebody that they didn't accept. For whatever reason, they didn't accept it. Most of the time, it was something we really didn't want to give. A sincere gift, whether money or a hug, your help or advice, is usually accepted graciously. Giving makes us better people.

I'm not talking about material things. I'm not talking money. I'm talking about gifts. I talking about flowers somebody picked from their garden. I'm talking about a really good hug. I'm talking about somebody that can tell a great story, somebody who helps cook or somebody who even offers. You know the person. You know the people. I told them not to do the dishes but they're doing them. They ask you if you need anything. They're caring. They're lavish with their love, they are great friends, good companions. Gosh, they bring so much to the party.

Giver or Taker?

Look in the mirror. Are you a giver or a taker. Give more of your love to others. Smile more. Hug more. Listen. Help. When you feel like you should do something, help with the dishes, get more wood for the fire. Find a way to help. Just do it. Give to the world. Give to yourself.

Hot Kisses and Cars

We all want to get invited back to the party. When somebody offers you a gift, take it. Say, "Thank you." That reminds me of my Dad. Dad told me, "When anybody offers you money in this life, always, take it and sincerely say, 'Thank you.'" My Grandpa Goldberg used to give me money whenever I saw him. I remember he'd have a huge wad of sweaty money, a hundred on the outside. I got into it a few times and discovered fifty ones on the inside. He was a wonderful man. That's my story and I'm sticking to it. His way to love was to give us some cash.

He did give great hugs and he kissed me. I kiss all my friends. Maybe that's where I learned it. He loved hot peppers; when he kissed me, my mouth burned!

My Father would give me anything in his power: motorcycle, clothes, cars. He even bought me a car when I graduated from high school. It was his way of giving, showing me love, his way of loving. I appreciate it. But, it isn't what I was looking for. I was looking for a hug. Don't get me wrong. Dad definitely loves me and I love him. It was just so different from my world.

Giving Open

My Mom's gifts were love and caring. She listened. She'd give anything she had of material goods. She gave of herself. She told me her fears. She told the truth. She was a free spirit. She wanted to heal the world. She still does. She's a giver in the most precious way.

Get Back On And Ride

Be generous — be giving. Look in the mirror. Clear your mind. What's it feel like to get a gift, a special gift, as when somebody comes up and says you mean so much to them and thank you for that? Give unconditionally. When you receive, be thankful. I gave you my heart — and you stomped on it. Ouch. Sometimes, life is hard. It's hurtful. We've all given gifts that were precious to us, but unappreciated. Remember the good gifts. Keep giving. Forgive those you gave gifts to, gifts that you gave and were stomped on. Hey, if you get bucked off, get back on. And ride, baby ride. Stay strong. Stay mentally tough. Remember the good, the positive. Give unconditionally. Be thankful. Be loving. Be a giver. Be generous.

It's Not That Easy!

It's not that easy. Yes. It is that easy! It's simple. We all know the difference between right and wrong. Yes it is just that easy. Smile. It's the first thing people notice about you. Write down a few things you do to can help others.

No Blue Ball

Ever want something special from somebody? Want them to give it to you so bad? My Grandfather was a blustering, opinionated, "I'm always right" kind of guy. He was impetuous. His sons did not feel accepted and loved by him. He was a man who showed very few emotions other than brashness: he was tough to be around.

Don, one of his sons, was going through therapy. My uncle was a tender, thoughtful child. He wanted his dad to listen to him, to be kind and caring, to recognize him. He didn't know if he really loved his dad or if his dad really loved him. While he was going through therapy, he had a dream.

Uncle Don tells the story like this:

His Dad Irv would reach into his pocket and say, "quarter" and flip the quarter out to him. He could tell what coin it was without looking at it. He would pull a dime out and say "dime" (yeah, the same Grandfather that always gave us cash when we saw him) and flip the dime to him.

In the dream, Don asked his Dad for some blue love. Irv pulled a purple marble out of his pocket. "I want some blue love, Dad." And Irv pulled a red marble out of his pocket. "No, Dad. I want blue love." Irv then pulled a green marble out of his pocket.

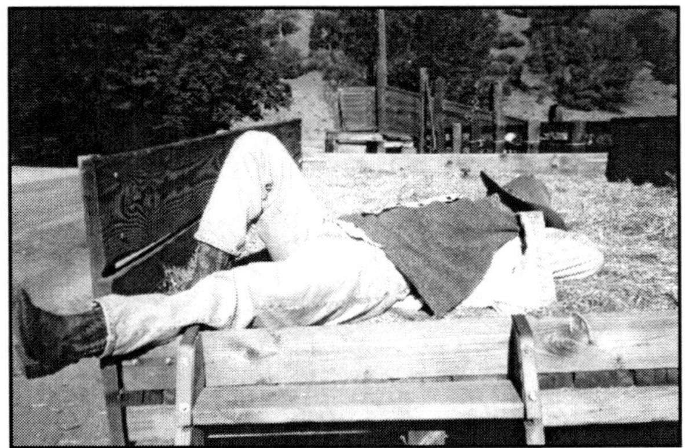

If You Get Bucked Off . . .

. . . Get Back On And Ride.

Then Irv fell over backwards. When he hit the ground, all of the marbles rolled out of his pocket. There were no blue marbles. He didn't have the blue love Don wanted. His Dad did not have it in him.

Get it? We knock ourselves out wanting things from people that they don't have. Forget it. Be a giver. Some people are just not capable of giving you what you really want from them. At what point do we give up? Usually, if we want something that bad from someone, it's our parent, our son, our daughter, our mate or our coach.

The Ring

Have you ever received a gift that's beautiful and special but it's not what you want? Not what you had in mind? Maybe the gift giver spent months picking it out, finding exactly what they thought was the right gift. When Richard was dating his wife Rhonda, they were discussing what type of rings they'd like. Richard told her exactly what he wanted: a gold band, plain, thin and simple. He described it perfectly, exactly the ring he wanted.

Rhonda shopped for months. She went to many different jewelry stores and fell in love with a ring that, in reality, was a lot nicer (diamonds throughout) than the one Richard had described.

She dressed up, took him to a special dinner, and bought him his favorite drink, which had a heart and two beautiful curly straws in it. He knew something was up. His heart was pounding. He was excited. Her heart was pounding. She was excited. She had tears in her eyes. They loved each other. They wanted to spend the rest of their lives together. They both held their breath as he pulled the ring from the drink.

"What the hell is this? This isn't what I wanted. This is all wrong. You know this is not the ring I wanted."

What a Dick!

She cried when she went home. She was trying to give him something so special — a piece of her heart — something she couldn't even afford. She was crushed. Richard was crushed. She returned the ring and got the one he wanted.

Both Hurt

This is a perfect example of giving something special and having it rejected. It hurts deeply. Who do you think was hurt more? Initially, Rhonda, but Richard learned that he had been wrong. He knew he handled it terribly which is why he told me this story. And that's why I'm telling you. Could he have handled it better? How about, "Thank you honey. It's so beautiful. It's nicer than anything I could have imagined."

In a sense Richard would be lying by saying this. But only a shallow person would see this as a lie because it is such a special gift; it means so much to her. He ruined the moment. He broke her heart. Yeah, it healed. He got the ring he wanted. I bet when he looks at it, he thinks about the other ring. Mom thinks we should give people what *they* want — not what *we* want to give. That's a point. Although, Pop always wanted to give what he wanted to give.

Love What You Get

So, be prepared to love what you get even if you don't get what you love. Did Rich change? He's doing his best. He can do better. So can the rest of us. Is it just that simple? Yeah. It truly is just that simple. The choice is yours: Happy? Or miserable? What do you choose?

Self Control

Sometimes we need to stop, take a quick breath and not say anything that hurts the other person or destroys the moment.

20

Food

In and out

As we're writing this, Mom mentioned *In and Out* when I said "burger." They make the best burgers, extra sauce, crispy fries. It's okay to spoil yourself once in a while. You need to feel good to look good. Food is love. Food is life. It's nurturing. Food is nourishment. Food is an art. Making food for others is love and caring. It tastes good. It's a way to share with others.

I Eat Too Much

Why do some people eat and eat and eat? Is it because they're hungry? Because it tastes good? Some people say, "I feel depressed, so I eat and eat. I eat too much, but I'm still hungry. I'm always hungry." You will feel so good to change what you put in your mouth. You will be healthy. This one thing will change your self esteem, will change your life, will change the way you feel about yourself and the way other people feel about you. I'm not saying you're a bad person because you're fat or skinny. I'll still love you. Are we really hungry? No. We don't eat because we're hungry. We eat because we are accustomed to our eating patterns. Food is an addiction.

Sharing The Eating Moment

It's my thyroid. It's my glands. I'm out of balance. I inherited it. It's my genes. Everyone in my family is overweight. I take after my grandfather. It was my childhood; they fed me too much. I'm not happy, so I eat. My mom put it in front of me. They encouraged me to eat, eat, eat. We all ate. We thought we were having fun — sharing the eating moment.

Do you ever stop to think, "I'm so overweight? Why can't I stop eating?" Well you can.

Clear Your Mind

Step back, clear your mind and think it over. You know the truth. You know it's unhealthy. You know when you look in the mirror — or down — you feel bad about yourself. You know it hinders you in every way: your self esteem, the way others see you, the way you see yourself, your love life, your exercise, your ability to look good, feel good, your ability to move, your longevity and your health. In every way, you are hindered by fat.

You're a Fat Person

Big people are big people. Fat people are fat people. What's the difference between fat and big? A fat person is overweight — that Milwaukee tumor! — fat thighs, fat arms, fat stomach, fat face, fat, fat, fat. A big person is big, not overweight, not obese. In our society, at least, in the USA, we have plenty of food. We have plenty of chocolate, cakes and donuts. Most have enough money to eat all that we want to eat. So, what's the problem? The truth is that we're weak.

Weak, Weak, Weak

Step back. Look in the mirror. Change today. Realize you eat for some other reason than hunger. Take a picture of an obese person and put it on your fridge. Find a picture of you when you were fit; you looked good in your bathing suit; in fact, you looked great! This is a sensitive subject, because fat people tell everybody and themselves "It's okay to be fat. I like being fat." It's a lie. It's a cop-out. It's abusive. It hurts you more than anybody else. Change. Realize the truth. Everyone must eat enough only to survive, not surround themselves with enlarged fat cells.

Be Strong

Yeah, it's hard, but how many times have you lost 40 pounds and gained it back in the same amount of time it took you to lose it? We're all bad. We're all good. We're just doing our best. Wait a minute. Is this my best? Can we do better? Can we feel better? Can we exercise? Absolutely, without question, you eat because it's an addiction. You eat because of whatever reason you lie to yourself to make it okay. Realize it is a lie. When is the time to stop eating — to feel better about yourself?

Tomorrow?

I'm going to start my diet tomorrow. You've already lost. Start now. How do you feel when you're fat? How do you feel when you're just right? When you're healthy, do you have more energy? Do you feel like dressing up? Looking good? Do you feel like going to the beach? Do you feel like wearing shorts? Do you feel like asking somebody to dance? How good do you feel when you look in the mirror and you like what you see?

Stop Making Excuses!

It feels great doesn't it? Stop making excuses. Start now. Be strong. Stop making excuses. Stop making excuses. It's a bad habit. No one can fix it but you. Only you have control over this. It's one of the few things in life that is totally up to you. Be strong. Start today. It's your Best Day Ever. It's just that simple. Be strong.

Skinny Minnies

I've focused on a fat or obese person but, in the same instance, it's just as pertinent to someone who is too skinny. What is too skinny? Look in the mirror. You know the person, the one that brings to mind, "Gosh, they need a burger." There are also those people who look great eating nothing but burgers and fries. That's their choice. It takes years and years from our lives to eat the wrong food. You know what's healthy. You know what's good for you. Eat right. Love food. Love yourself. Change today. It's up to you, no one else. Make no more excuses. Start now. None of us is perfect. We're all good. We're all bad. Do your best. No. Do better.

You're the Boss

Whatever excuse you give yourself, whether it's love, a bad thyroid gland, etc., etc., stop lying to yourself. You'll love yourself more when you look in the mirror and smile. You'll be easier to hug. You'll make love more. Excuses are a lie. You're just fat. I'm just fat. Mom's just fat. Dad's just fat. Pop's just fat. I could eat better. I'm going to start today. I already like what I see in the mirror, but I can do better. I'm going to start now. What about you? No excuses. It's up to you. You're in charge. You're the boss. Look in the mirror. Hey, let's all change. It's just that simple. Be strong. Be strong. I know it's hard, but it's time to stop making excuses and time to feel better about yourself.

Strong Love

As we write, we cry, we grow, we learn, and see that we already know the truth. We're just weak. We have a choice. I have a choice. You have a choice. Choose to live long. Choose to look good. Be strong. Start now. I love you. Mom loves you. Richard loves you. Love yourself XOXOXOXOXOXOXOXOXOXOXOX!

Food is Love?

"Eating is a substitute for love." Ever hear that? It's an excuse. Food has nothing to do with love. I know I said that food is love and it is, but eating is not a substitute for love. It's just another excuse to eat too much. Look in the mirror. Is that love? Mom says fat people want a whole lot of love. I want a whole lot of love. You want a whole lot of love. Mom wants a whole lot of love. Dad wants a whole lot of love.

My Father

My Father loves to eat. He loves to cook. Heck, who doesn't like anything sautéed in butter and garlic. Who doesn't like really good cream sauce? I love to eat. I love to cook. I have a scale in my house. I get on it every day. When I gain weight, I don't eat the stuff I know is not the right thing to eat. I started talking about my Father. The one thing I remember most about my time with my Father, which was limited to about a month every summer, was that I would sit up on a stool and cook with him.

It's still a special part of our relationship. We talk about recipes and dishes. He's overweight, not obese. He goes on diets and loses up to 30 pounds in 30 days. I bet he's lost 5000 pounds in his life! He always gains it back as fast as he loses it, which is unhealthy. When he had his first heart attack and bypass, I stayed with him for six weeks. I cooked for him; we cooked together. We cooked healthy things that tasted good. We went for walks. The day I left, he smothered his pancakes in butter.

I talked to him over and over about this subject. After his last surgery, he hadn't been back to the doctor in about six months. I called the doctor. He said, "Your dad is stubborn, hard to talk to, doesn't listen, and doesn't show up for his appointments. He's a lot like my dad!"

Live Long, Dad!

I drove down to see him and took him to the doctor.

Dad says, "Adam, I'm going to die with a good taste in my mouth."

"Dad, I have one child. I want you to be there for her. I want you to help her learn to be a good cook. Change is good, Dad. You know what to do. It's just that simple."

Dad looks great. He eats right. I don't think my conversation changed him but the doctor told him if he continued abusing his body, eating the wrong food and not exercising, he'd live less than a year; if he took care of himself, he said he'd live for a decade or more. Live, Dad. Play with my children. Change today. Change now. It's just that simple.

People and Mice

Have you ever gone without food for the day, fasted? Do you think this is unhealthy? Do you think your body needs that food? For some people, yes we do, for those people who are in perfect harmony with their bodies. We all know who they are. We say, "Oh they're so lucky. They have great metabolism." Most studies show that being slender or underweight enables people (and mice) to live longer.

21
___

Health and Healing

Investigate — follow your heart

As you go through life, as life moves through you, you will encounter illnesses. When a serious illness has been diagnosed, more than likely, it's not going to go away by itself. Whatever the illness, explore all types of healing opportunities: traditional or alternative medicine, whatever you find that appeals to you. Western medicine is wonderful. It can do amazing things; more often than not, you'll probably get good advice. I encourage you to get more advice, to learn, to investigate, to explore different types of healing: homeopathic, alternative medicine, vitamin therapy, fasts, anything that causes your spirit to leap in joy, then, follow your heart.

The Other's Illness

If it's somebody else's heart and they make a decision you don't agree with, give them your advice when it's warranted. Ultimately, they'll do whatever they want. It's their decision. It's their life. Support them and love them. Nourish them. Give a piece of yourself to them even if you don't agree with their decision. More than anything, they need your understanding and support.

Picture Them Healed

Honor them in whatever way comes to you. Be with them. Picture them surrounded by light. Picture them well. Picture them healed. *Your* faith might heal them!

Standard Procedure

I remember when my mother was diagnosed with cancer. We all knew it was wrong. She was so full of life. I was always sure she would live forever. They prescribed a mastectomy followed by chemotherapy and radiation. We all pressured her to do what the doctors wanted. The oncologist told my Pop, "If it was my wife, I'd have her in there today."

Mom searched her whole life for spirituality, for balance, for her self, for love, for truth. Initially, she listened to the doctors and got a mastectomy. In fact, she had three surgeries in four weeks: two biopsies and the mastectomy. "It was tough!" she told us. She was heading towards conventional treatment of cancer. But, in the way which is her way, she started searching. She found alternatives she thought were better.

I stayed with Mom when she had surgery. We talked a lot. I had no experience with this condition. I wanted her to do what the doctor said, but I didn't tell her that. What I did was support her in what she decided to do. This is what she found. This is what she did.

Vacuumed Right In!

I was really shocked when I was told I had cancer as just weeks before, I was told convincingly, *This is much ado about nothing.* Then: the mammogram, the suspicions, the biopsy and the advice to have a mastectomy. In my case, they discovered tiny, little cancer cells in the milk ducts of the breast. (I personally believe these are common and normal in older females.) Even though there was no typical lump, 'they' wanted to cut off the breast.

I believed 'they' knew what they were doing and, that somehow, losing this traitorous breast would make me healthier or heal something awful.

It wasn't until *after* the surgery that I read that whatever treatment they prescribe, nothing is guaranteed to solve the problem, prolong life or increase your health. No one told me that *before* the surgery.

Too Late — Drats!

At the time, an approachable medical specialist and expert on breast cancer was on the staff at the Medical Center. In one of her books, she identified optimum treatment for breast cancer for a woman of my age (60). It didn't jibe with the advice given by the oncologist. I called her. She was in her garden and graciously took my weekend call.

I told her what the oncologist wanted to do. She said they had to support their families, pay for the Mercedes and put their kids through college. It's a business. She also said the only treatment medicine had found for cancer was slash, poison and burn. In other words, cut, chemo and radiation were all they had and they couldn't guarantee the effects of any of these damaging procedures.

Wow. If they don't know what they are doing, who does?

We, my husband and I, went to the library and there, picked up a book *Spontaneous Healing* by Andrew Weill. I was so impressed by the analogy of cleaning a stream: take a few poisons out of it and it clears itself in 24 hours. Dr. Weill compared this to the wonderful ability of the body to heal itself. That seemed right to me. I believed.

The Cure For Any Cancer

A little lady Hulda Clark studied microbiology. She discovered that any time she found a cancer cell, she found two accompaniments: fasciolopsis (liver fluke) and propyl alcohol. Her theory was to rid your body of the parasite and propyl alcohol. Additionally, she recommended the removal of toxins and contaminates from your environment and your body. This liberates the immune system to attack any cancer cells roaming around. Pop read Clark's book. He, a practical businessman, agreed with her logic.

I studied and read. And found in the American Cancer Society's *Textbook of Clinical Oncology** on page 49 that two researchers wrote: the epidemiology of cancer has been found to be associated with a parasite, namely, the liver fluke! Wow! Rid yourself of parasites and be cured of cancer? That would sure ruin an entire medical industry, now, wouldn't it? I have never read any publicity about the liver fluke being responsible for cancer. Why?

Follow Your Heart

I still didn't quite know what to do. There is enormous pressure to stay in the *system,* to believe in the doctors, to believe they are

---

*American Cancer Society's *Textbook of Clinical Oncology,* SECOND EDITION, 1995, on page 49, "SEVERAL PARASITIC INFECTIONS ARE ASSOCIATED epideiologically with cancer. Among these are liver flukes and blood flukes."

right, that they care about us, that they know how to heal us. Most persons, friends and relatives, thought I was nuts not to do what the doctors wanted.

A most wonderful friend, author of *The Alpha Book on Cancer,* Brent Ryder, told me and I'll never forget these freeing and loving words, "Johana, keep gathering information until you know in your heart what is right for you." I did just that. And, I discovered that, whenever I thought of alternative procedures: Dr. Clark, diet, prayer, meditation, special teas, enemas, cleansing, joy leapt in my spirit; when I considered chemo, radiation, I went dead inside. I told Pop, "I am going to follow the joy." And, he supported me in every way!

Dr. Clark and Alternatives

We did all the things Dr. Clark said to do in her book *The Cure for All Cancers.* Two times, we went to Tiajuana (where she was exiled to conduct her treatment) to be tested to see if we had rid my body of the parasites and contaminates. The second time, we tested clean. We were elated.

Another book is *Cancer Battle Plan.* I drank special teas and special fasts. Took many vitamins. Every morning we prayed Psalm 91 — that God will cover me with his wings and provide refuge from the deadly pestilence. I was prayed for at our church — many times.

Any time I heard about or read any alternative treatment that appealed to my heart and spirit, I went for it.

The QXCI

One of those treatments is an electrically based program, called the QXCI. One of Adam's friends had a pain in her chest. Finally, after a year of wondering what was hurting her, they discovered a plate size lymphoma. She earnestly believes the QXCI helped her to heal; these treatments don't heal, they balance your body and your body heals. I had these treatments and even went to Oregon to receive these benefits. She also credits some chemotherapy.

"I'm Not Having This"

At some point, I don't know when and I wasn't conscious of it at the time but, in a deep, deep part of my being, and with my entire self, I announced to myself and to the cancer cells, *'I'm not having this.'* I think this deep, inner decision instructs the body, the mind, the T Cells, to go to war on your behalf and lick this thing. I never claimed having it. I never called it *mine.* I announced I didn't have it. *'Be Gone'!*

Healed!

Part of refusing the chemo was that I thought it would kill me; I *knew* it would kill me. Also, I thought, if I am going to die of cancer, I want to have a joyful blast between now and then.

I pronounced myself healed. I called Adam and told him, "Honey, I'm healed." Adam said, "Wow, Mom. That's fabulous. That's great." I believe in my Mom but I still wasn't sure she was healed!

I also decided (following my heart) that, if I *was* going to die, I wanted to do all the things I love: write, sing, help my husband, be with my kids, be with my grandkids, play tennis — the way I love doing them as long as I could and then, a week or so before, prepare to — and then choose to stop breathing.

That was seven years ago. I am now, as we are writing this 72 years young. Still kicking. Playing on the tennis team with ladies who take their toddlers into child care. I tell them, "Call me, 'Mom'"

"Your Faith Has Healed You"

My husband Elmer was a brick. He stood by me and was 100 percent helpful and supportive. I didn't tell anyone except people I knew were 100 percent for me. I didn't want any negative thoughts about me out there in the world. I wanted all the positive help I could get. And my husband did that. Also, my kids. They love me and I love them.

I am a thankful person. I am a believing person. I thank God for healing me and for all the loving, faithful persons who prayed for me. What healed me? Was it Dr. Clark's program? Was it the prayers? Was it faith? Was it the enemas, the teas, the vitamins, the QXCI, the determination? I don't know. God knows. I just thank God for healing me and do whatever I can to pass my experience along to others. I think the most valuable thing is to do in your heart what is right for you. Spirit, Mind, Body. Go figure! . . . End of Mom's experience.

Another Story — Chris Johnson

Back to Adam. I have another friend, Chris Johnson. He had a backache. It became increasingly painful. He went to the doctor, had an MRI, x-rays, etc. etc. The diagnosis was that he needed to have an operation. He went to three doctors. Each prescribed an operation.

At the time, his family doctor was on vacation for three weeks. Chris decided to wait and talk to this doctor who had known him for years. His family doctor told him that the problem that was showing up on the MRI and the x-rays had been with Dave his entire life. It was a bump that had been there since he was a kid! Dave's doctor said he was fatigued and needed rest! That did the job.

Maxine's Story

Our friend Maxine was diagnosed with a "very large hiatal hernia." She had noticed when doing the yoga shoulder stand that something would slide up into her chest. She'd stand quickly, raise her arms and it would slide back down. She didn't know she had a 'sliding hernia,' a stomach that was sliding up into her chest.

Finally, it became so hurtful that she could only eat small portions at a time. The doctor recommended surgery. The surgeon was an expert and practiced a procedure using laparoscopic — from outside in — to pull that stomach back down where it belonged and to stitch the torn tissues that were allowing it to migrate.

Maxine had the surgery. It was a very painful operation. She was elated after the surgery. The surgeon told her she could do whatever she wanted. She was healed. About three months after, she felt it tear again; about six months later, she knew the stomach had again pushed through the torn esophageal tissues. Maxine was disappointed. Fortunately, insurance paid for the $50,000 surgery but, now, what alternatives were left?

Maxine "discovered" David Marquis, a chiropractor and a gifted healer. David manually manipulated the stomach, deftly pulling it back down into its proper position and told Maxine: "Never tighten your abdomen. Leave it loose because your muscles can push the stomach up through the tear."

She has been able to resume activities and remembers to keep a loose abdomen. Of course, she wishes she had first gone to David rather than suffer the pain of the surgery. But, she is glad to have found him and glad to know that if the stomach pushes through again, she has an alternative, a hope for treatment.

Later, after visiting Dr. James Stephens, a Naturopathic Doctor at the Ozark Health Center in Cassville, Missouri, she learned to manually draw the stomach down. More freedom.

Alternatives

Alternative medicine, alternative medicine! As you can see from the above testimonies, you have to be persistent and search and search. You'll find a circle of dedicated individuals who can help. Anything nature provided is better than a great deal of things the doctors prescribe. We have to remember that, if they didn't do surgery, a lot of people would be without jobs. If we can heal ourselves with food and vitamins, what happens to them?

Western Medicine

As I said in the beginning, there is a place for the wonderful discoveries and techniques of Western medicine. You just have to pick your spots!

The anecdotal experiences of individuals herein shared are not intended to provide medical advice or to be a substitute for medical recommendations by physicians or other health care providers.

22

Death and Dying

Hanging with the Great Spirit

What Happens When We Stop Breathing?

Most of us know someone close to us who has stopped breathing. What do you think happens when we die? Do we die? Does our body die? Do we have a spirit? Does our spirit die? Does our spirit live forever? Do we go to another place? Is it a good place or a bad place? Everyone in the world has different beliefs, different religions, differing theories on what happens to us when we stop breathing.

Good Place or Bad?

We've all seen movies or heard individuals share their experiences about dying, seeing the light, traveling to another realm. Does that really happen? How do we know? Are we reincarnated? Do we go to heaven or whatever place it is your religion or your belief says? If we're bad, do we go to the bad place? Who decides whether we're good or bad?

Your Beliefs Are Your Beliefs

I really don't think there is a definitive answer to these questions. Each person has his or her beliefs depending upon their religion, what they've been taught by their parents or their environment. Each religion, each person defines death in a different way. Are we really forgiven? Is everyone forgiven? Are only the Christians forgiven? Are only the Jews forgiven?

Karma, One Good Term Deserves Another!

I'm not sure about a lot of things but I am sure that the Higher Spirit, God, Perfect Love would not be this judgmental. If we do go to heaven, all the good people: the Buddhists, the Muslims, the holy, the good, the kind, the loving, the honest, the pure, the noble, the people who have given their lives for a cause they believe in — I could go on forever — would be saved, that is, go to heaven, are forgiven. I'm positive they'd be on the same ride — get to go, too. Or, get to be reborn or whatever it is that happens when your spirit goes to the good place, whether that means reincarnated or to heaven.

I believe that you get what you give, karma is the term that comes to mind. One good term deserves another! Could a God that is so beautiful and so good that gives us all the beautiful things that we experience: our children, our lives, our happiness, butterflies, nature, the ocean, sunshine — does this God condemn the bad people or forgive them? All we've done so far is ask an assortment of questions to which no one has answers. You might have the answer for yourself, but your answer will not apply to everyone.

We don't all have the same beliefs or the same religions. This is what I believe, what I feel in my heart, what's real for me.

Afraid to Stop Breathing

We all have friends who fear death and fear dying. If we knew the answer, if I could say, "We're all reincarnated, we all go to heaven or whatever place your religion says you go to if you're good or holy," we wouldn't have that scared feeling when someone we know dies or when we think about the end of our lives, when we stop breathing. I believe there's no death without life, there's no good without bad, there's no love without hate. The worst it could be is like sleeping without dreaming. Do you like to sleep? Sounds peaceful, doesn't it? No more worries. No more hurt. Does that mean there's no more love, no more happiness?

When We Stop Breathing

When I said, no good without bad, I was trying to get across is that, when we stop breathing in this life, our body definitely dies. Even if we're not reincarnated, our spirit or our essence lives on. I don't think our spirit ever dies. Whether or not the spirit goes to heaven or a special place, our spirit continues in another way. That spirit lives in the people we've influenced. I think the best description of this is the letter I wrote to my Mom on her 70th birthday.

August 16, 2000

"Hi Moma. I love you sooo much. I can't begin to put it in words. The best way I can express my love to you is to tell you that I feel the same way you do when you look at me.

"All that I am is because of you. All the joy I feel and the love I share with the world, my passions for friends and family, sports, life, animals, God, people, is all what you gave me. What a Gift! As long as I live, you will always be alive because you have given so much of yourself to me.

"There is so much of you in my heart. And I, in turn, will share this love and those special gifts with my friends and family, because you would have it no other way!

"And they will give them to their family and friends and they will give them to their family and friends.

"You will live forever in my family — until the end of time. XOXOXOXOXOXO I love you."

Abu

"That's Not Moma"

As we were writing this, Mom started to tear up and I asked her what was going on. She told me this story about when her mom passed on.

The Three Sisters and their Mother

"When Moma died, Marilyn, Cathie and I went to view the body before the memorial service. They used to do that in the old days, to look at the person for the last time, to say, 'Goodbye, we'll miss you.' So, in we tiptoed, awe inspired, a little afraid to see our Mother's body — what it would be like. We stepped up to the casket and there she was, in her familiar, neat, soft gray dress, hands folded across her breast. We peered in, almost holding our breaths. Finally, Marilyn broke the spell, 'That's not Moma.'"

We three sisters agreed. "Nope, that body, that form, was not our Mother."

Mixed With His Hands

I remember when my grandfather Grandpa Goldberg died. As he was dying, I was talking to him and I was crying. He said, "Adam don't cry. If I die today, don't cry. Don't worry. I've lived 10 lifetimes in one. Don't grieve. Celebrate my life."

Wow! When I think about him, I smile, remembering his many wonderful qualities. I think about him often. His spirit lives in me; his spirit lives in his children. I don't remember his faults. I remember his wonderful kisses. I remember his generosity. I remember his salads: oil and vinegar, salami and cheese always mixed with his hands. I remember his passion. His spirit will forever live in me. I'll make his salad for my kids and they'll make it for theirs.

That Lopsided Grin?

We know each of us dies. There's no escaping it. No life without death. Will these words help you when you think about death, think about your own mortality — your friend or family member who's dying? I think so. I hope so. Be strong for them. Remember the good. Feel their love. Sometimes a special thing happens that reminds us of somebody that's passed. Maybe, your parent's facial expression, a term, that unique laugh, a lopsided grin, a picture or a salad?

The Only Real Thing in Life is Love!

Share with them. Don't wait. Make sure they know you love

them. Make sure they know how much they love you! Tell them anything that you've always wanted to tell them. Don't protect. Don't hold back. Forgive them and let them forgive you. Hug them a lot. Kiss them a lot. Tell them how precious they are. The only thing that's really real in life is love. Think about it. It's that simple.

Remember the Smiles

If they're already gone and you feel guilty or incomplete about your relationship with them, if you cared about them enough to feel guilty or incomplete, know that they cared about you as much as you cared about them. Even if you never got a chance to talk about it, they love you and care about you as much as you care about them. And, even if they never forgave you or you never forgave them, in their heart and in your heart you both know what a special relationship you had. They've already forgiven you. Time to forgive yourself. Remember the good, remember the love, remember the smiles, remember the laughter. Are you smiling? I bet they are.

Why Not Go With It?

Their spirit will live forever in everyone they've touched and, who knows, maybe they were born again the minute after their spirit left?

Are they in a better place? We don't know, so why not go with it? Maybe you do know. Honor them in whatever way you think appropriate. And you can be sure that, when you pass, when you stop breathing, the worst it can be is like sleeping without dreaming and, without a shadow of a doubt, your spirit will live on forever, one way or another.

See the truth. If you're born again, beautiful; if you go to heaven, that would be heavenly; if you go to hell, you deserve it.

Part of the Good

There's no good without bad. Start being part of the good today. Start being part of the good now! See the truth. Dwell on the beauty. Love everyone. Be loved by everyone. You know you have a choice. You want to be good, or bad? Nobody's perfect. Maybe I should change my name to "Nobody" — probably not the right spot for humor.

Thanks for the Ability to Understand

I've lived 10 lifetimes in one; if I die today, I'm content. I'm happy. I can make a great salad. I know I'll live forever in the hearts of my friends and family, in my children's hearts and souls and their children's hearts and souls and in their children's friends. Today, I am alive. I'm breathing. It's the most beautiful day ever. Thanks for life. Thanks for the ability to understand. Thanks for the truth. The truth is I choose to be happy. The truth is I choose to live and smile. It's my Best Day Ever. But, I'm thinking tomorrow might just be a little better.

I'd Like to be a Falcon

I choose to remember all the wonderful things and all the wonderful people, some breathing, some not breathing, that have touched me in my life. It's just that simple, genius. Be happy. Smile.

I'd Like to be a Falcon

Laugh. Love. Remember the good. It's just that simple. And, when the time comes for me to choose to stop breathing, whatever's going to happen will happen. We might as well smile. I'm thinking I'm going to be hanging with the Great Spirit and, if I'm reincarnated, I'd like to be a falcon.

Are you Afraid of Dying

Eventually, your day to stop breathing will come. Does that petrify you? Are you afraid of dying? Anne, my friend, thinks about it and she is very troubled and scared. When I asked her why, she says, "Well, I'll be dead."

When she said this, I asked, "What do you think happens when you die?"

"Well, I'll stop breathing and I'll die."

"I know that part, Annie, but what scares you?"

"Because I don't know what happens when we die."

"What do you think happens?"

I could see the hurt, the worry, the fear in her eyes.

She said meekly, "I think we go to heaven."

"Well, do you think heaven will be a bad place?"

"No, I think it would be a good place."

"If you truly believe you're going to heaven, heaven would be the most beautiful place in the world. You'd be hanging with the Great Spirit. Right?"

" I guess so, but I'm not positive what happens to us when we die."

I said, "Anne, the very worst scenario is that it could be like sleeping without dreaming."

She asked, "Well, what do you think happens to us when we die?"

"I'm not sure. I love to sleep. No worries. No pressure. It's peaceful. But, this is what I believe. I believe I'll stop breathing and my body, yes, will die. Who knows, actually, some of it might live in somebody else. I'm a donor. For a time but, eventually, all my body parts will be dead. I'm sure my spirit, my essence will live forever one way or another."

She said, "What do you mean 'live forever one way or another'?"

"I believe my spirit will live on, hanging out and partying with the Great Spirit. It's possible our spirits are reborn — again and again. As a matter of fact, it's probable. I always wanted to fly — maybe I'll be a falcon. Are you still scared?"

She said, "Yes. I don't know what's going to happen when I die."

"Well, you've got a choice. You can choose to think or believe that you're going to die and it's bad and terrible; or, you can believe that it's going to be better, that it's going to be peaceful. You have a choice — good or bad."

"You make it sound so simple, Adam."

"It is simple. You have a choice to see the good in everything, to dwell on the good, to dwell on the beauty or to see the negative and the wrong. Why would anyone choose to see the bad when it's so simple, nurturing, comforting and positive to see the good?"

Is Tom Already Dead?

"Remember when your brother Tom was in Florida? Hurricane Hugo was hitting the Florida coast. You called me crying, saying your mother had just called and that she was sobbing and telling you that your brother might be right in the middle of the eye of the storm."

Anne was crying, sobbing, scared to death, feeling the grief of her dead brother.

I was petrified. "Is Tom really dead?"

You said, "Well, we don't know. We haven't talked to him. Mom's been trying to call and can't get through."

"Anne, go to your mother's. I'm coming right over."

When I got there, they were both hysterical. They were glued to the television, watching Hugo destroy Florida.

Sobbing, crying, hysterically, they told me Tom was right in the worse part of the storm.

I turned the TV off and begged them to sit down and quiet down.

Anne said, "But, Tommy could be dead. He's in the worst part of the storm!"

"Let's just be quiet for five minutes and take a couple of deep breaths. I want you to listen to me. Tom is probably fine. He knew the hurricane was coming. He had time to prepare. You haven't talked with him, have you? He might not even be in Florida."

Helen said, "But we don't know. He might be in the middle of the storm."

"He's a smart guy. He's probably just fine."

They said in unison, "You don't know that."

"No, I don't know that but, if you were in Florida and you had 48 hours notice that a huge hurricane was coming, would you stay there? Would you find a safe place? Of course you would. Why should we assume that he's dead, hurt or injured if we have no idea, no information. Let's assume that he's fine. Let's believe everything is okay."

"Yeah, but he could be hurt bad; he could even be dead."

"Yes, but why assume he's dead? If you want to assume he's dead, that's your choice. Why would you choose to assume he's dead without any information that would lead you in that direction?

"The TV said it was 95 percent evacuated, so the chances of him being fine are 95 percent; the chances of him being not dead, but there are five percent. The changes of him being dead are less than one percent! Tom's fine. Let's not bury him until he dies."

I hugged Helen and Anne a lot and tried to be comforting and smothered them with love and positive energy.

Hurricane Hugo Party

I stayed with them until we heard from Tom.

"Tom, what's up? How's everything? You're alive!

"Dude, it was unbelievable. We had a party. We got a bunch of food and alcohol. We had this cement room at the house where we were staying. It was really cool — like a bomb shelter. We had a Hurricane Hugo party. It was a great party. The place is really torn up. We are all going out to see if we can help."

"Well, I'm glad you're not dead. Let's do lunch. I love you. See you soon."

Helen and Anne were elated. I was elated. Yeah, I was sure he was okay but there was still that one percent!

Why assume the worst when we have no information and we have a choice to assume, not just to assume, but to believe and dwell on the positive and the good?

They Even Show Us Their Dog!

In our society, we dwell on, in fact, we magnify anything bad or wrong. The front page of the newspaper tells about the deaths, the murders, the robberies, the man-eating diseases. The television seeks them out, magnifies them, talks about every part of it, shows us the pictures of the dead, shows us the murderers, shows us the friends of the murderers, the parents of the murderers, shows us the people who have been robbed. They show us the man-eating disease, the man with his flesh gone, dead. It was the only person who had ever died from this disease but, they focus on it; they tell us the plague is here. They show us their family, their grief. Heck, they even show us their dog.

And, when we go out to work or to play, everybody talks about it. They live it, they share it, they grieve for the people. The next day in the paper, if there wasn't a worst tragedy, they magnify it, they dissect it, they expand on every aspect of the murders, the disease, the robberies and then everybody talks about the new information.

Who's Buying It?

Unfortunately, this probably won't change. This is how they sell their papers; get the best TV ratings. Is it their fault? Think about it. Who are they selling it to? Who's buying it? Who's watching it? Who's talking about it?

We are. You are. I am. It's what we choose to dwell on. It's what the world talks about. Did you hear about so and so? Did you see this? Did you see that? We magnify it; we make the stories even better.

You have a choice. You have a choice to dwell on the good — to talk about the good. To dwell on the beauty. To actually be the good, be the beauty. Share the good, share the beauty. We could even magnify it — make the stories even better. My friend Jeff says I sound like a greeting card, "You never want to talk about the bad stuff. Whenever I bring it up, you ask me, 'Is it going to be sunny tomorrow?' Bad stuff happens, Adam, murder, robberies, the man-eating disease. It's our world. Why won't you talk about it?"

"I'll talk about it. I realize there are bad things in the world, you know, murders, robberies, the man-eating disease. I want to talk about it if I can fix it or help in any way. But I don't want to share it with my friends. I don't want to dwell on it. It's not my world. I don't want to see their dead bodies; I'd like to hug their friends and family. I'd like to help. I'd like to stop the murders, stop the robberies and, if I had an opportunity to help make things better, to stop the bad people, I do and I will.

"It's not what I want to dwell on, talk about, share with my friends, seek out. I don't want to talk about it over and over again, gossip about it. I have a choice. You have a choice. I choose to dwell on the good things in life. The beautiful things, the positive, the sunshine, the things that make us smile, the good stuff. You have a choice too."

"You sound like a greeting card, Adam."

"Hey, did you see the waves today. The swell's up. I've got three days off. I'll come up tomorrow and we'll play ball. I bet it's beautiful at your house. Was it sunny today? I'll bring my book and we'll just chill."

Beauty, All Around

We are all free to choose what we want to think about — what our focus is. We have a choice to see the good, see the beauty, share it with our friends, live it and feel it. Smile. It's contagious. It's the first thing people notice about you. What do you choose? Do you choose to dwell on the evil? Do you seek it out so you can drag it through your conversations with your friends? You have a choice. What do you choose? Yes. It really is that simple, genius!

We're Perfect Again

Mom asks, "What does this have to do with death and dying? You know, Honey, the stuff about the bad news?"

"Mom, think about it. It's an analogy about life, about our society, about death and dying. If we don't know what's going to happen in any situation or happen to our friends, why assume it's bad? Why concentrate our thoughts on it?"

It's all good. It's my Best Day Ever. How's your day?

When we were born, we were perfect. When we stop breathing, we get to start over. We're perfect again.

23
___

Spirit-Religion-Judgment

Talk to me — saving Adam

What is Spirituality and what is Religion? I believe they are two completely separate things.

DICTIONARY DEFINITION RELIGION: System of faith and worship. A personal awareness or conviction of the existence of a supreme being or of supernatural powers or influences, controlling one's humanity or nature. An organized body of believers. Personal commitment to and serving of God in accordance with sacred writings or teachers.

DICTIONARY DEFINITION SPIRITUALITY: Spirit is the breath of life, the animating principal of life giving and inspiring power. Spirit is the opposite of material. The vital principal in man coming as a gift from God and providing personality with its inward structure, dynamic drive and creative responses. Joined in spirit.

SPIRIT

Spirituality

Spirituality is that relationship you have with Something that can't be explained with words. A man witnessed two perfect rainbows. He wept with incredible joy, saying, "It's so beautiful, it's so beautiful." It's that Something we talk to when we see that perfect sunset and we give thanks for the beauty. It's feeling, emotion, pure love, guidance, the right answers and comfort. It's that rosy glow we feel when we think about how blessed we are. It's when we are hurt and we ask the precious Something for help.

I refer to that Something, the Great Spirit, Mother Nature, that warm, rosy feeling, ultimate love, perfect Guidance as God. I'm not saying it's a man or a woman. Maybe it's something we can't put into words. I don't want to offend you. You may have a different name, maybe you can't name it, whatever name or feeling you put to it is right for you. I'm sure there are a hundred terms; I don't know them all. It's a sensitive subject because it's spiritual, it's holy, and it's perfect. Whatever word you use for her is okay and it's the right term for you. The term I use is God.

It's a Glow

It's a feeling. It's comfort. It's joy. It's guidance. It's knowing the difference between doing the right thing and doing the wrong thing. It's a glow you see in people when they are at their very best or when they kiss their baby for the first time.

When someone we love dies and we need help, we ask for help — not human help from our friends or loved ones — but help from that perfect place. When we're lost at sea in a tiny boat or clinging to a piece of driftwood, it's that person we pray to for help and rescue. It's forgiveness. It's patience. It's warmth. It's comfort. It's support. It's holy. It's perfect. It's a role model. It's what we strive to be as humans: perfect, holy, and Godlike.

Our Guardian Angel

We have a Guardian Angel who watches over us. I am blessed to have an intimate relationship with God. I talk to the Great Spirit every day, every hour. I thank that Spirit for the sunrise, for where I live, for my family and my friends. I can't tell you how I know there is a God. Well, maybe I can.

What's His Name?

In every religion, in every society, there's a term, a name each culture uses to describe their God. I believe there's one God. God is love, spirit, light and the creator. God is powerful. God is pure, God is beautiful. I think God speaks through people, really special people, and gives them callings and guidance.

We Are Forgiven

It's very comforting to know that even though we make mistakes, do bad things, even though we know we have done wrong, we are yet forgiven, we're still loved. Some people go to a church to gather together with other people and worship and sing songs to God; some people don't go to church. People worship their God in many different ways. I think he's the same God regardless of the name we use. I don't go to church very often. I worship God in my own way. I see Him in nature. I see Him in people.

Talk to Me

If we talk directly to the Spirit, we can know it hasn't been tainted, watered down or edited. We don't have to wait 40 years for its wisdom to be written down. We don't have to wonder if someone *got it right.* Have you ever played the phone game? Get ten people in a room, one of them tells a story to the person next to them. That person tells it to the person next to them and so on and so on and so forth. Then, the last person tells the story that they heard to every one. By the time it gets to the tenth person, there is very little left of the original story.

Now, take that same game and add to it greed, and a desire for power. Who wrote all these books? Was it God? Was it the Great Spirit? Was it individuals? I am not saying they are wrong; I am not saying that they are right. Maybe they were inspired by the Great Spirit. But, why not talk to God or the Goddess or the Great Spirit directly? This is such a sensitive subject; spirituality is personal. It's between you and the Great Spirit.

Call Him Up

The Great Spirit is everywhere: the sun, the stars, mother earth, waiting for you to speak directly. One on one. Personal. Go right to the top. If you had an opportunity to ask the president a question, you might be able to talk to a congressman or maybe the vice president; but, if you had the opportunity to talk to the Man, wouldn't you? Of course you would. The answers would be there — answers that come directly from the Source. The questions would be *your* questions; the answers would be exactly what you needed to know, exactly what you needed help with.

This is so hard to write because I don't want to taint your beliefs with my beliefs about who or what the Great Spirit is. Whatever it is for you, it is right. Go to the source, face to face. Get the answers right, make sure your questions are right. Don't have someone do it for you.

Religious leaders give you their interpretation of God, of forgiveness, of spirituality, tell you how to worship, how to repent, tell you what you are doing wrong, what you are doing right. I am not saying they are wrong, I am not saying they are right.

Think about it, why not speak directly to the Great Spirit? It's there waiting, She's listening. He's listening. He has answers, compassion, love. She has warmth, beauty, tenderness, encouragement, passion, a love with no equal. It has forgiveness, strength, and perseverance.

Share your love with other people: sing, dance and share your experiences. To pray or worship or whatever you do together, is good and comforting and powerful. It's what the Great Spirit wants.

We Can't Thank God Enough

We don't say "Thank you" enough for what we have. We ask and pray for our home, our family, the beautiful landscapes and we forget to say, "Thank you." I know how blessed I've been. I thank Him for everything.

Are You Sure?

Am I sure there's a God? Yes. Are you sure? I can't say that for you; it may be a Goddess. Whatever name you use for that spiritual being is what I call **God**. I use **karma** a lot in my day-to-day life. I love this term. It means you get what you give. If you're good, good will come to you; if you're bad, you get what you deserve.

RELIGION

We Never Did Anything Jewish

I really don't know that much about religion. Mine is with the Jewish and the Christian religions. My father was Jewish. When

I was young, I said I was Jewish — I thought it was my race. My father always said he was Jewish, but we never did anything Jewish. The only time I remember going to Synagogue was for my cousins' bar mitzvahs. They got a lot of cash. I always wanted one.

Crackers and Juice

I went to a wedding in a Catholic Church. One of my friends was getting married. We sang some great songs. Octo played the sax. Sy made everybody laugh. Scotty wore sandals with his tux. The priest never smiled. He showed no emotion. He didn't seem to be singing with us. I didn't get any crackers or juice. When we left, I asked Mary,

"Why didn't I get any crackers or juice?"

"You have to be baptized and go to confession."

"Heck, you're not Catholic and received some."

"I used to go to the Catholic Church. I have been baptized and I have been to confession, so that makes it okay."

"So, the rule is that I'm not holy enough to participate. I know there is a part in the Bible about the bread and the wine; but I don't remember hearing about the confession."

A Guy Behind a Screen

I don't understand confession. Why would I talk to some guy behind a screen when I could talk directly to the Great Spirit?

Let's say I was the adviser to the king and I wanted more power and money. I might find a way to get everybody in the kingdom to tell me all the worst things they ever did in their lives. Once they told me all the terrible things they did, I would tell them they would be forgiven — for a price. I would be the most powerful man in the kingdom, wouldn't I? If the king told me, I'd be more powerful than he. And I'd be rich too. They'd be obligated to give me money. They would have to be loyal. I would know every bad deed they'd ever done. They would never get out of line — good followers that had a lot of trouble thinking for themselves.

Religion can be a wonderful, a really good spiritual thing. I think all are good if they make you feel better, help you dwell on the good things in life, help you to be a better person and make you smile and laugh more. I apologize if I have offended you, but, why wouldn't you talk directly to God? Why wouldn't you ask for His forgiveness? His help and guidance? Do you think that priest is a little more powerful? More holy? A better listener? Do you think that priest is more understanding, more compassionate, has more forgiveness, more loving than God???

Son, Read the Bible

When I was 15, my Mom asked me to read the Bible; she said it was important. I asked her where to read it; she had only been reading it a week or two, so she said,

"Anywhere you want."

I opened it and it said, *If you have sinned, take an unspotted goat to the altar.* "Mom, do we have any unspotted goats."

Richard and the Bible College

My brother Richard was going to Law School at USC. While he was attending the University, he went to a church on the hill in Los Gatos called *Youth for Jesus.* He was caught up in it. It became his whole life. He quit USC, studied at their bible college. It changed him, some good, and some bad.

He went to the Marshall Islands and South America on a staysail schooner called the Rose of Sharon. They distributed Bibles and presented their bible program.

He Just Didn't Look Right

I remember seeing him after he returned and he just didn't look right. He was working for the church, sometimes 14 to 16 hours a day. I remember driving with him from Los Angeles to Santa Cruz. We left at six o'clock, drove until midnight.

"Let's go say hello to Mom. You can spend the night."

"I won't talk with Mom."

"Rich, why not?"

"She's a sinner."

"I thought we were all sinners. Rich, you sound awfully judgmental."

Basically, our entire conversation was about me coming to church and getting saved. I couldn't believe he didn't want to talk to Mom anymore.

"Heathens and Sinners"

The next weekend he was back in town. He called and invited me to church on the hill in Los Gatos. Almost all Richard's friends were now in the church. I missed him and knew it was a good way to spend time with him. So, I went.

Everybody was really nice. I loved the singing. The preacher started to preach. He was telling all the kids they weren't doing their best. He was harsh. He was staring into the audience, especially at me: "Heathens and sinners, come forward and be saved." I didn't go. A lot did. They were crying. Many were speaking in tongues. They were laying hands on people, praying for them. He stared at me a lot.

I Want My Brother Back

I didn't like the service. I didn't think it was holy. The people were so judgmental. After the service, the preacher came up to me,

"Adam, you're a sinner. You need to repent and ask the Lord into your heart and ask Him to forgive you."

"How do you know this?"

"You're not saved. It is obvious to me."

"Who are you to judge me? I thought that was God's job."

The preacher got angry. "If you don't leave right now, I'll have you removed."

"Tom, are you perfect? Are you holy?"

When I left, I told him, "You are a really bad role model. You and this church took my brother Richard away from my family and now he won't talk to our Mother."

Tom became so angry I thought we might get into a fight. I was nice and calm inside and really wanted my brother back. I left. Richard wouldn't go with me. I sobbed as I drove home by myself. My brother is my closest friend

A Knock on the Door

The pastor stayed up all night and came into my house at 7:00 o'clock in the morning. He knocked on the door. He had tears in his eyes as he asked me to forgive him. He had been thinking it over!

I told him, "Absolutely not. You took my brother away from our family. I don't think you are a good leader. You want me to give you my forgiveness? I'm hurt and I'm bitter. I still don't think you are a good person. I don't think you are holy."

Tom asked, "Adam, would you pray with me?"

I told him, "No, but I'll pray for you." He left.

That day, I drove back up to the church where Richard was going to the Bible College. By the way, he studied for four years, and never received any degree that means anything in the education world. That's too harsh, he did it because it was the right thing for him to do at that time in his life. A degree is just a piece of paper. Back to the story. I knocked on the door.

They asked, "Who is it?" I said, "Adam, Richard's brother."

"We're busy now."

The door was locked.

"If you don't let me in, I'll knock the door down."

I knocked the door down.

I was crying in the middle of their school saying, "I want my brother back. How can this be good for him? Or, for Richard's family? I don't believe God would like this. You are deceived."

I cried. I sobbed. I tore my shirt off. My brother left with me. We went to Mom's house. He told her he loved her and that he was sorry.

Religious, Not Spiritual

Of course, I forgave them. Later, they found out that the head of the church was sleeping with a teenage girl in the church. I think the end came when I kicked the door down. A lot of eyes were opened.

I forgave Pastor Tom. Tom called and came by my house on several occasions. I didn't return his calls. I would not answer the door. I came home from school and he was waiting in my driveway. He had been talking to God and knew he had been *religious* and not *spiritual.* He wanted to make it right, he wanted to thank me, and he wanted to tell me that the leader of the church had tainted his religious path and the church

Actually, the church did a lot of good, more good than bad. Thirty to forty of our closest friends, people we'd grown up with, were in the church. A lot of bad apples changed when they came to believe in God. For some, it saved their lives. I can think of several of the rowdy party animals that fought, beat up policemen, etc., that now are loving fathers and husbands and a lot better people. I think it helped my brother a lot more than it hurt him. He's been a youth pastor and a Bible teacher and has been in other churches. Richard doesn't go to church much anymore, but he is *very* spiritual.

The Dancing Goldbergs

Richard was the Best Man at our wedding. It was a holy day. Richard said, "Adam became a flame of fire, with healing flowing around him as he talks to Dad, Pop, and his friends." I was holding people's faces in my hands and looking into their eyes. I wanted so desperately to make sure they heard every word, felt what I was

Our Wedding Day

feeling. We all danced and danced and danced. They called us *The Dancing Goldbergs.*

Flowed Like a River

The Spirit was flowing like a river. It was beautiful. It was holy. It was spiritual. It was good. It was healing. We didn't pass the basket. I think this analogy says a lot about religion and spirituality. And it shows our wedding day, which was spiritual. It was partly religion. It was structured. We said, "I do," which is something that has gone on with churches for centuries. It was good. It was pure. There was nobody's distorted views, no prejudices, no wrongs, We didn't worship according to the program. It was a really perfect display of church, religion and spirituality.

A Great Way to Play With God

I'm using religions I am familiar with. I'm telling you what spirituality is to me. Of course your experiences will vary, be different. I think that some religions are spiritual and good. And, it is good to share your spirituality with others. Be spiritual in your own way. I'm a person who walks with God. I am a friend of the Goddess. We're tight. When I was a kid my Mom took me Sufi dancing. It was very holy, very spiritual, praising God, dancing, bowing and laughing. Now, that was a great way to share our spirituality. It was a great way to play with God.

JUDGMENT

Don't Judge Lest Ye Be Judged

Don't throw rocks if you live in a glass house. Let he who has not sinned cast the first stone. I think in today's society, in our world, there is way too much judging going on.

Judgment is Part of our Life

If you do something wrong, you suffer the consequences. You get what you deserve. We sit around and talk about somebody that did something awful. We decide that they are terrible people. We judge them. We judge people every day. He is a great baseball player. She is a great softball player. That team sucks. That is the best team in the league. They should go to jail. They should get rid of that loser. Joe's not guilty. You think?

Are We Always Right When Someone Is Wrong?

Are we always right when we decide that someone is wrong? Are we always right when we decide somebody is not wrong? Obviously not. We are human. We make poor decisions. We don't like to be judged. We usually don't agree with the judgment that has been decreed upon us.

The Court System

In our society we need the court system, the legal system. It's not perfect. Hey, it was designed by humans! Lawyers help us in the process. Ouch! Wait, I am being judgmental. There is good and bad in all of us.

Everybody knows the difference between right and wrong. *We* know when we have done something wrong. We know when we have done something right. Judgment has its place. It can be a really good thing. If your job is to judge, be the best you can. Every judge has made a mistake. Every judge has made a wrong decision, put someone who is innocent behind bars. People who have done bad things need to be stopped from hurting others: robbing, stealing, whatever it is that they did. I don't know how to help our legal system improve. I think it is a good system, not perfect, but good.

We Are The Judge

What I am talking about is you and me deciding somebody else is bad or wrong — making judgments upon them. Examples — You're not saved, you are going to hell. That guy is a terrible father. My son's a loser. My daughter's a loser. My parents are terrible parents. I'm right; they're wrong.

Rhonda's Story

Rhonda is my sister-in-law, and my sister in every sense of the word. She told me this story. She was a checker at a natural foods store. They were very busy and she was the only checker. There was a long line and the lady she was checking insisted on being helped out to the car with her groceries. She made such a scene that Rhonda left her station to help her out to her car. When Rhonda returned to her counter, she was talking to the other people in line about what a rude and insensitive person that lady was. "I can't believe there are such

Rhonda's Story

selfish people like that in the world." The other people in the store chimed in and agreed. "She doesn't care about the rest of us." (Guilty)

Just then, the lady returned with big tears in her eyes. "I'm so sorry. I apologize. I did not mean to put you out. I came back in because I felt guilty. I just had open heart surgery and I am not supposed to lift anything. I should have told you earlier but it is hard for me to share my pain with others. Please forgive me".

Judge Yourself First

If you must judge people, be sure to judge yourself first. Make sure you know the truth. Even then, you might be wrong. Who are we to judge? Who are you to judge? It's easy to see other peoples' faults. It is hard to see our own. See the good in people. Heck, the Iranians love their children too.

From Cover to Cover

You read the story about my brother's church; no that's wrong. That's not *his* church; that was a time in his life when he was learning. We were trying to write about another subject, but we couldn't get off this one.

My brother knows the Bible from cover to cover. There was a time in his life, when he went everywhere with his Bible. I remember he came to my football game with his Bible and his friends from church. He was trying to save everybody. He was doing what he knew, not what he thought but, what he *knew* was right. He was judging people. He was deciding who was "saved".

My relationship with Richard is special; he is my best friend; he is my role model; he's honest; he is holy and yet, he would judge everybody but me. At that time in his life, he told my Mother she was a sinner (Mom says he was right about that!) and he didn't want to see her. He was so judgmental, but he never judged me. Instead, he told me about God, he cried but, he never judged me. He did judge the rest of the world.

Saving Adam

I'll never forget a ride I had with Richard and his brother-in-law, who was also in the church on the hill. Richard and I were going to see our Father in Mexico and drop David (brother-in-law) off in Bakersfield.

David started talking about saving me. He told me I was a sinner and that I should repent for my sins. He told me I was going to hell. I know enough about the Bible and the Christian religion to know that God is supposed to judge people. I said "Who the hell are you to judge me?" I was bitter, I didn't like the church they were in. My experiences with the church were not very pleasant. I thought the church was taking my brother away from my family and me. (My brother says, "They were.") I was hurt. I was bitter.

"David, are you perfect?" He answered, "No, but I am saved and you are going to hell." I wanted to hit him. I probably would have if it weren't for Richard.

A Friend of God

This is a terrible part of organized religion, so judgmental, so opinionated. I was sitting at the bar at Stars Restaurant, talking to my friend Owen Henry. He introduced me to a guy at the bar, a regular, whose name was Chris. In conversation, Owen asked how the book was going. I told him, "It is amazing. When I sit down to write, it just comes out perfect. It is almost like, it's not my book. Sometimes I feel like the Great Spirit is writing it." Chris said, "Oh, are you a Christian?" I said, "I don't know, but I am a friend of God. I talk to Him and thank Him every day."

He said, "Where do you go to church?"

God is Everywhere

I said, "Everywhere."

Chris said, "What? How could you go to church everywhere?"

"I sense God everywhere. I thank Him. I thank Him for the sunshine. I thank him when I wake up in the morning. I thank him for my friends. I thank him for my wife. I thank him for my daughter. I thank him for my family."

Please forgive me if *him* is not the right term for God to you. I don't know if "it" is a him; I don't know if "it" is a her; I don't know if "it" is a person. But I know that she's there, or maybe he's there.

Back to the story. I told him my favorite thing about the Christian religion was Easter. I love Easter. There might be better stuff in there but the fact that he gave his Son so that we can be forgiven was very special to me because I know that I need to be forgiven. He told me in his opinionated way what Easter was really about.

"Adam, are you saved?"

"Saved? What do you mean when you ask, 'Am I saved?'"

"The only way to God is to ask Jesus into your heart. That is the only way to God and if you don't ask Jesus in, you are going to hell."

"How is it that you are supposed to judge people? Isn't God supposed to be our judge?"

"Yes, but, the only way to heaven is to acknowledge Jesus as Lord and repent from your sins."

I said to him, "How do you know?"

"I know".

"How?" He said, "I got saved from church and it is in the Bible and I read it."

What If They Didn't Have the Right Book?

I asked him, "If God is so great as my God, our God, would He not let somebody into heaven if they were holy, spiritual. For instance, I don't know what they call them, but there are people that don't step on a blade of grass, they won't kill an ant, they devote their lives in prayer to God, good people, honest people, spiritual people, who maybe never even heard about Jesus, from a different culture from a different world; you are trying to tell me that these people will go to hell? Do you think God would be this judgmental?

"Do you think God would not love somebody, would not forgive somebody who was good, who was honest, loving, tender, who was spiritual? Who was just a good person. Somebody with great 'karma' would be denied heaven? Sent to hell? Because they didn't have the right book?

"Chris, who wrote the Bible?"

"It was written by God. Well, it was written by men, but it was the Word of God."

"Chris, ever play that game where you tell people in a room a story and they tell ten people, then the last person tells them what they heard?"

Silence.

"Yes, but the Bible is different."

The Truth

Don't get me wrong I am not saying that the Bible isn't the **truth**. I am not that judgmental. But I don't believe and I don't know how anybody else can believe that because they call their goddess or god or supreme being by a different name that they are not holy and that they are going to hell.

God Is

God is love. God is mother. God is father. God is in everything. God is good. God forgives us. Thank you God for forgiving us. When I say who or what God is, I don't know that I am right about a lot of things but, I am sure that God is not that judgmental. I am sure that God has forgiven us.

My last name is Goldberg. With the exception of my brother and me, they (the rest of the Goldbergs) all follow a faith that does not recognize Jesus as God. But, in the Bible it says "— and so all Israel shall be saved" [Romans 11:26]. So, let's see, God will forgive the people that crucified his son, put him to death, and don't believe that he is their savior. They never asked him into their heart, they rejected him and killed him and yet, they get to go to heaven?

God Loves

If you are good, you're good. I believe that God loves us all. He is the Father of all fathers the Mother of all mothers. While I am writing, I said, "Forgive me, Lord, if some of this is wrong." He did! She did! It did! I love the term **karma.** To me, it means you reap what you sow, you get what you deserve. Good people deserve good things; good people get what they deserve. Bad people get what they deserve. Are you good? Or bad? Yes, you are both. Are you forgiven? Do you forgive? I don't believe that you can be forgiven unless you, in turn, forgive.

Let God Be the Judge

Remember, God judges, people don't. Spirituality is good. My brother says he is no longer in the judging business. He has been in churches, an assistant pastor, a missionary, a Bible school teacher and has a degree, a piece of paper that says he completed his religious training. Following are Richard's observations on church and religion.

Richard Defines Religion

"Adam asked me to define religion and spirituality, see above. Amen!"

A Holy Bow

Every day of our lives, we can learn something new. We can grow as a person. Writing this book forces growth — to look at myself. Things that we were positive were right are positively wrong. We were sure our thoughts and beliefs were right ?????????!!!!!!!! I was more judgmental than I thought! I had decided some religions were wrong, religions that I knew nothing about. Change is inevitable; growth is optional.

I can't stop thinking about Sufi dancing with Mom. It was a little like square dancing only people were so happy. Square dancing is fun. Everyone smiles, giggles and laughs, but Sufi dancing had some extra ingredients. We smiled and sang the songs with passion. I always wanted to go. I have not Sufi danced in over thirty years, but I remember every word of the songs we sang. We bowed to one another. A holy bow.

A Flavor for Each Person

Do you like ice cream? What a question! Everyone likes ice cream. What's your favorite? Mine is mocha almond fudge. I order it every time. I have not tried them all. Matter of fact, I have only sampled a few. Without question, mocha almond fudge is the right one for me. I wrote a book report about it, saw it on TV. Heck, everyone knows that mocha almond fudge is the best. It's a proven fact. It's heavenly!

What is your favorite flavor? I love ice cream. It's my favorite food. Just talking about it makes me smile and crave a banana split with lots of flavors.

My Mom's not here but I know exactly what she would get. She has me try it. She wants to share it with anyone who takes the slightest interest in ice cream. She wants to share it with the world.

Mom's having a malt. Not a milk shake, but a malt. French vanilla ice cream, a spoonful of that malt stuff and a tiny bit of chocolate — a little bit so that it's just the right color. That's perfect. Mom says, "Try it."

A flavor for everyone — right, good and yummy. What's your favorite?

24

Violence and War

Kills a part of our spirit

We know people in our day-to-day lives who are mean, violent and abusive. Meanness is hard to deal with. This is tough. Mean people suck! It is a terrible flaw. I am not sure "flaw" is the right term. It is cruelty, harshness and brutality. It is wicked.

Two Black Eyes

When I was 13, my friend came over with two black eyes and bruised ribs. His father beat him up on a regular basis. He came home drunk or in a bad mood, hit his wife and my friend. He cried and tried to tell me what he did wrong to make his father hit him. He even went so far as to say it was his fault. He made excuses for his father.

No Excuse for Abuse!

I don't believe there is **any** excuse for hitting a child or spouse. How do you forgive this? Should we excuse the abuse? Say, that his dad hit him so he hit his kids and they hit their kids? I can't.

Creating Fear

Ever go to a sporting event and see some macho d*@# head dad yelling at his kid because he made a mistake? Because he made a bad throw? Screaming at his kid that it was his fault they lost? Slapping him? It is hard for me to forgive this type of cruelty. It is an ongoing part of that child's life. He is afraid he is going to do something wrong; afraid he's going to be abused; fearful that his mother is going to be abused, beaten, hit, tortured verbally and physically.

What to Do?

What advice can I give about this subject? I want to hug you. I want to beat up that guy that is slapping his kid around. Turn the other cheek? I think it is a great term. Maybe for a grown up. At this point, my advice is to get them out of your life. "Yeah, Adam, but it is my father." Wow! Tough, tough, tough! What should I do? What should I tell you to do? I can't answer this question for you. I can tell you what I think I would do.

Do we give them another chance? Yeah, maybe, one. Protect yourself. Get a restraining order. Don't make excuses for their harsh behavior. Do whatever is best for you. Get help. Get away from them. This is a very hard subject for me. I love you. Love yourself. *It's not your fault.*

Consciously Objecting

I agree in general with the term, **turn the other cheek,** that, is, don't react to another's wrong with a wrong of your own. Stay balanced. But at some point in time, I believe there is also a time to fight. I was talking to my friend's father who was a marine in Vietnam. We were talking about war. He wanted his son to be in the marines.

I told him, "If there was a war, I would be a conscientious objector."

He said, "Adam, I know you pretty well. Let me ask you a question. I am not sure exactly what 'conscientious objector' means but you are saying that if you were in a war and had to kill somebody, you wouldn't or couldn't do it. Is that right?

"Let me ask you this, if somebody came into your house and was going to kill your mother and brother or sister, and you had a gun in your hand, now, if you could kill him or watch him kill your family, would you pull the trigger?"

"Yeah I would."

I abhor violence and yet, in this situation, I would choose violence. I would choose to kill.

When is Killing a Person Right?

When is killing a person a viable alternative for not getting along? For what reason? A person becoming a terrorist? Being a different race? Having another religion? Holding beliefs unlike yours?

I believe more people have been killed in the name of religion, than all other wars combined. If you were drafted, would you go to war? Only you can answer this question. For the right reasons, I believe we all would. Not all, most of us would. If you answer that question about your family by saying *no*, I guess you would not go to war. I can't think of anybody I know that would answer *no* to that question.

Persuade the Common People

War sucks. Some wars need to be fought, but very, very few. In a war, the opposition believes their cause is worth dying for. The enemy's perception is different from ours; they believe they are right; we believe we are right. When you saw the people burning our flag in Afghanistan, did you want to kill them? Would that end the war? No! A few terrible people do terrible things. Most wars are fought because someone in authority: a king, president, general or religious leader is manipulating news, information to arouse the citizens to war. They want the other people to be like them: to wear what they wear, talk like they talk, pray the same prayers. Oh, yeah, and pay those taxes and that ten percent!

Those in authority have to persuade the common people, us, to fight for them. If we sent the people in authority to fight the war — in the front line — we would have fewer wars. Let's say they had to be the first people to hit the beach, or lead the charge, I wonder if then they would be in favor of that war.

Wag the Dog

Did you see the movie *Wag the Dog*? The leaders create or design a war? They involved the masses through showing pictures of innocent children being killed, hateful people burning our flag. Those who watched TV and read the paper were behind this war 100 percent, "Let's get those bastards. Nuke them."

They convince them that those others, the opponents, are bad and evil; that whatever they are doing is wrong, terribly wrong. They bring the great power of morality, good and bad, into the situation and sell that to the common person.

In some sense, this is reality. When I say *reality,* I mean that we don't really know the people we're going to war with. We only know what we are told, what we are shown on television and what we read in the paper.

Thank You For Protecting Us

I don't want to offend anybody who fought in a war — or to say any war you were in was unjust. You're the bravest. You're the strongest. You were willing to give your life for your country or for a cause you believe is just. Thank you. Thank you for protecting us. Thank you for protecting me. Thank you for risking your life.

Viet Nam was a war that became unpopular. Nobody thanked you when you came home. You felt unappreciated. You offered your life. Some of you gave your lives. You went to war for us. You did what you thought was right. With the information you were provided, it was right. I don't know if it was right or wrong.

What we missed in all of this is that we failed to separate the right and wrongs of the war with honoring the men and women who fought for us.

With the media and the information that we were initially provided, we thought it was just. Was it just? I don't know. I'm not saying it is or it isn't. I really don't know that much about it and from what I can tell, nobody else does either.

War is Evil

The nature of war is evil. Those who fought in a war carry the war with them as part of their lives. It is painful. They are forever changed. They've experienced evil; they experienced death. They killed. They've seen the faces of the people they've killed. They are traumatized.

Such Brave Souls

War kills a part of our spirit. It doesn't just wound it, it kills it. We send our children, our mothers and fathers to war. They go, such brave souls. They go to defend our honor. They go to save us. They go because it's the right thing to do. I thank you all even if you believe the war that you fought or that your children fought or that your parents fought was wrong, It doesn't change the fact that you went at that time because you believed that it was a just cause, that it was the right thing to do.

Do You Feel Deceived?

Do you feel deceived? If you feel deceived, you probably were. It's not your fault. You're a beautiful, brave person. You followed your orders. You gave your life or part of your life. Thank you. It's not your fault; it's not their fault. Did your mom or dad come home? Your son or child? Your husband or wife and they weren't the same person? War killed a piece of you too. It's an experience that I can't fix — that they can't fix. They deal with it because they don't have a choice. You deal with it because you love that person.

You must forgive your enemies; you must forgive yourself. War kills us all. We've all done terrible things we'll always remember, we'll never forget. This is something that's hard to just let go or move on from. It killed a little piece of each one of us. It killed a little piece of each one of you and a little piece of me.

One Man — Two Groups

One day, Jesus went to a group of people. He told them he loved them. They loved him back. He was godlike. He was the healer. He cared about them. They received him with open arms. They believed what he said was the truth. They believed he was the Messiah. I believe the people loved him because they saw the love he had for them.

One day, Jesus went to another group of people with love in his heart and in his eyes. He went there to save them with the truth. It was what he believed, what he knew was right. He was going to save all of them. He told them he was their Messiah. He came to help them, to show them the truth. He told them he loved them. He told them God loved them. Their response to this man was to drive him away and to kill him, "Let's not just kill him, let's crucify him!"

I believe this group wanted to kill him because they were going to lose their power, their money, their esteem, their authority, and their high place in that society. They didn't want to lose their ten percent!

This story shows two different peoples' reaction to the same thing: one loved and one crucified.

I'm not saying that he was or wasn't the Messiah. I'm not saying that whatever religion you practice is wrong. You may not believe there is a god at all. And I'm not saying that your god, goddess, spirit, saint, whomever it is that you pray to is wrong. That's your choice. I don't want to judge you.

Know What the War is For

In every war, in every fight, in every disagreement, the people fighting the fight, fighting the war or having the debate believe they are right. The people who decided to crucify him weren't the ones who crucified him. They, the leaders, had told the people such terrible things about Jesus that they believed it to be a just cause to kill him. Did they know him? No. If I ever have to go to war, kill somebody or be willing to kill somebody or be killed, I guarantee you I'll know what it's for. What do you think?

World War II

How do people feel about World War II? They feel patriotic. They feel like we won a war that had to be fought. Everybody in the United States was behind it. It was just. It was the right thing to do. It was time to go to war. War, unfortunately, in our society, is part of our lives. Of course, I wish we'd never had to go to war. We all do. But, we can't always turn the other cheek. Sometimes, sadly, war is the right thing to do.

All We Have Is Today, Now!

Life is good. Life is glorious. Life is wonderful. Life is hard. No good without bad; no bad without good; no life without death; no freedom without opposition. You can't change yesterday; you can't go back and redo it. It's already done. Forgive yourself. Forgive your family. Forgive your friends. Forgive your enemies. All we have is today.

How's your day? Is it your **best day ever**? It's the only day that means anything. Smile. Love. Hug people. Hug your friends. Be good. Be strong. I love you. We all love you. Feel the love. Feel the joy. You have a choice. You have a choice whether to dwell on the bad, terrible things that have happened or to dwell on the good. I do believe they need to be talked about and processed. But, you can let go of it. You can move on. You can smile again. You can see beauty. You can love yourself; you can love your enemies. The opposition loves their children; their mothers, their fathers love them. They were brave. They were fighting a cause they believed to be just. Maybe some of them didn't believe their cause was just, but they didn't have a choice, i.e., go fight or die.

See the Good

They were brave. They gave their lives for a cause. They killed for a cause. I don't know what their cause was. I'm not going to judge whether it was right or wrong. It's time to forgive them. It's time to forgive yourself. It's time to hug your mother or father. It's time to hug your children. It's up to you.

Stop making excuses. Whatever situation you're in, no matter how good or bad, you have a choice. You have a choice to be happy, a choice to love, a choice to let others love you. It's up to you. Nobody else. Start now. See the good. See the beauty. Dwell on the good. Dwell on the beauty. Fix yourself. Fix your friends. Fix what you can fix. You still have a choice. Choose the good. How's your day? It's your **best day ever!** It's the only one you've got! Is it just that simple? Yeah. XOXOXOXOXOXOXOXOXOX HUGS AND KISSES. It's never too late!

25

Racism

A scar on our souls

I don't say anything about anybody or any race that I wouldn't say in front of them. Do we all have preconceived pictures in our minds of a person's character because of the color of their skin, the shape of their eyes, their accent, the kind of car they drive, the way they dress, where they live? Are we all racists? I think so. I tell myself that I am not a racist. In our society, I think it's almost impossible to not have some preconceived feeling about one race or another.

Every County But America

When we think about racism and we say we are not racists, we know it's a lie. My heritage is Hungarian, Irish, English, Scot and American Indian. I think that's the only part of me that's really American! We're from every country but America! The only real Americans are the American Indians. And yet, we believe that we are Americans. I was born in America. But, with the exception of a little bit of Cherokee Indian, my heritage lies elsewhere.

My Grandfather

I remember going to the airport with my Grandfather, my Father's Father, and he yelled at an African American gentleman, "Hey boy, come here and get my bags." I almost died. I felt so bad. What do I do? I was 13 years old. I went up to the man and apologized for my Grandfather. I told him, "There's nothing I can say to take away the hurt in your eyes."

My Grandfather says it is his generation. I can't accept that. He's a racist. He used to tell me (he's gone, now), "I have lots of black friends." But it still bothered me whenever I was with him. We spent a lot of time in Mexico. My Grandfather had a ranch there. He hated Mexicans too!

"Grandpa, can't they all just be people? Can you meet somebody regardless of their color, regardless of the shape of their eyes and regard them as simply human beings? And then decide if you like them?"

Good question for everyone in the world!

What is an American?

What is an American? A white person born in the USA? Is it a black, brown, yellow, orange, pink person? No. It's an Indian. It's a Cherokee, Chumash, Apache, Navajo and the multitudes of other tribes who inhabited this beautiful land before *we* came!

Black and White

We don't like the term "white". Whites aren't truly white. Or anywhere near white; they are usually shades of brown/tan/peach/cream. Blacks aren't truly black; they are usually bronze/tan/brown. We hate all these terms: black, white, brown, African American, and Caucasian. We need new terms to describe who we are, or, do we? We're all human beings.

Birds of a Feather

Have you ever heard that expression *birds of a feather flock together*? In black and white society, generally, the whites are considered to be the most prejudice. Yet, African Americans are also as prejudice as Caucasians. Grouped around outstanding African Americans are generally more African Americans. Grouped around outstanding European Americans are generally more European Americans. I hope this doesn't piss John Thompson off, but since he's always talking about racism in sports, I'd like to ask him how many white guys started or played for him at Georgetown during his career. I'm not saying he's a bad person or more racist than anyone else. But I wonder.

Dad and Racism

My Father is a racist. He actually said that African Americans were better off because we made them slaves and brought them to the United States of America. Otherwise, they would still be in the jungle. It so infuriated me I said to him? "Would you think along those same lines about the Jews, that they would be better off because Hitler killed them, make lamps out of their skin, stuffed pillows with their hair; because, in turn, it made the Israelis the third most powerful nation in the world?"

My Dad is a Jew and he got very angry with me because he thought I was so out of line — and yet I told him "What's the difference? The whites came to Africa, killed people, stole children, wives, husbands, shackled and bonded them, whipped and beat them and made them do whatever they wanted them to do, took them from their family and their lives. How is that different from what Hitler did to your people?" He said, "You're being ridiculous and I am not a racist."

What About You?

What about you? How do you feel about Afghanistan? Do you think if you went there, you could make friends? I'm sure you could. Some of us would blame everyone of that color or nation for the actions of a few terrible people. I love this line in the Beetle's song, "The Russians love their children too." When we saw them burn the American flag and say, "Kill the Americans. Kill the Americans," do you wonder why they said that?

They were raised to think and believe a certain way. We believe the media, we believe the television, we believe the newspapers. I don't know that they have the type of media we have, but what do you think was on their local television, what do you think was in their newspapers? The truth is: they are not all Osama bin Ladens and we are not all Osama bin Ladens either.

What Can We Do?

What can we do? We have to realize and accept that we are all a bit racist. That's like looking behind that *Mask* (Chapter 26) to see who we really are. In every place, there are good people and there are bad people. There's no life without death, no good without bad, no winning without losing. There are good people of every color; there are bad people of every color. There are good people in every part of the world regardless of race and there are bad people in every part of the world regardless of race.

Why not just meet someone or see someone and wait until we get to know them before we decide we don't like them or we like them?

Gerrard

I played football my senior year in high school. We had a ball boy. His name was Gerrard Allen. We were really tight. He loved to come and play. He loved sports. Gerrard was adopted by a white family. Gerrard's not sure of his origin but he's definitely African American.

I was coming out of the shower. Gerrard, covered with mud was crying as he walked up to the locker room. I asked, "Gerrard, what happened?" He said, "Scotty threw me in the mud puddle and called me a nigger." Now, Scotty was the quarterback. He had blond hair and drove a Porsche. Naturally, I went to the locker room and pulled Scotty, butt naked out of the shower and beat the stuffings (Mom changed my original word!) out of him in the middle of the campus quad.

Gerrard became a dentist. Dr. Allen was one of the Best Men in my wedding.

We play on a basketball team together. Gerrard is super sensitive about racism. When an older guy said, "Boy, that was a great shot." Gerrard Allen got mad and left because he was afraid he was going to hit the guy. I don't think Gerrard did anything wrong because there is so much racism in the world. His feelings are justified. Whether the older guy meant "Boy" to be belittling, I don't know.

Riot in Los Angeles

I was talking with a friend about the riot in Los Angeles. Melissa said, after that happened, she had negative feelings about black people. I asked, "Why do you think they did that? Was it just because the cops beat up Rodney King?" I don't think so. I think it was years of persecution, years of racism, racism, racism, and people like my Grandfather and my Father.

I have loved and played sports all of my life. Mom said I had unique experiences and had so many friends from another race because of my sports background. "Mom, they're all just people. They're no different from me and you. Just putting them in the term 'them' is racist."

It's US

In reality, it is **us**. We're all the same — some handsome, some pretty, some young, some old, some dark, some light. We're all human beings. There is no **us.** There is no **them.** There is no way to tell if someone is a good person or nice person, a bad person or mean person by the pigmentation of their skin or the shape of their eyes — the only way to tell is to get to know them.

At Mount Hermon

While we were writing this, Mom told me a story. We lived right next to a Christian retreat, Mt. Hermon. Mom was going for a walk and heard beautiful singing. She went inside. She was the only one there without a great tan. When they opened the door, "I was loved into the middle of them. They all stepped back and made an aisle for me, as if it were planned. They put me right in the front with their honored speakers. I didn't know anyone but soon we were all singing and crying together. This beautiful young girl came up to me, put her arm next to mine and said, 'When we get to heaven, this won't be there.'"

(Mom wept as she told me this story.)

When she came home she told us (Richard and me), "I think we have black blood in our veins."

Richard became very excited, jumped up and down, saying, "I knew it. I knew it. That's why I can dance so well and Adam is such a good basketball player."

Look in the Mirror

Who wins? Who loses? It's all bad. It's all wrong. Who's going to change it? And, how do we change? Go look in the mirror. We need to stop blaming our upbringing, our parents, our society, and just do what's right — just **see the truth in things.** Do what's right. See who we are. See who they are. Take responsibility for yourself. Choose to be good, Choose to change. Choose to make a difference. Choose to love.

Gerrard on Racism

I was really excited for Gerrard to read the chapter on Racism, I thought he was going to like it. Wrong. When he read it, he was hurt. We talked a lot. It is a subject that he doesn't just talk or write about. He lives it. He carries it in his heart, mind and soul. "Adam, you don't understand racism. Not everyone is a racist."

This is close to Gerrard's literal definition of prejudice:

1. *The members of one race believe they are superior to other races.*
2. *Discriminatory or abusive behavior towards members of another race.*

Reverse Racism

I really started to think about it. Gerrard said, "There's no such thing as reverse racism." I argued my point, "What is the difference between Georgetown having all black players, black coaches and no whites ones and another team having all white, players and coaches? Either whites or blacks can be racists."

Gerrard's Story

The white people created racism here in America. Our ancestors bought and sold people. Let us say there is a small island somewhere and there are two different clans, one on each side of the island. The more powerful clad raids the other and kills the warriors, takes the women and children and makes them slaves.

The difference is huge. The difference is terrible. They took the women to be their wives. They had children with them. Those children became a part of their society. If the king took the prettiest one and had the child, that child might become the prince. Eventually, the slaves could become royalty. The workers became accepted as part of that clan. They married the king's daughters and they married the king's sons. They entered into their society.

In our country, not long ago, if an African American man got a white woman pregnant, he would be killed. He would never be seen as an equal. He was considered to be inferior. This is racism.

Times are changing. We are changing and doing a lot better about racism.

Perry, Georgia

Racism is improved but isn't dead. I was working in Perry, Georgia. Ed, one of the guys I was working with was from Macon; we were on our way to a barbecue at his house, Ed is a black guy. We drove past a little league field: ten diamonds, tower, lights, scoreboards, beautiful fields. Ed said, "Look at that." The fields were full, full of white people, not one black person was in the crowd.

Ten miles later there was three dirt fields, the fields were full, not one white person in the crowd. I could not believe it, total segregation. I looked over at Ed expecting to see a reaction, there was none. He was used to it. It was part of his life. A painful reality. I have never lived it. I have just written about it.

Gerrard Lives It

I have just talked about it. Gerrard lives it. While we were talking, I said, "I would never say the **n** word, you know the one." Gerry said, "Yes you did, you said it to me."

"Gerry, I have never said that word to you."

"Adam, we were on the balcony at the Crows Nest. We were talking about having a big boat and going to see the world. And you said 'We won't have to do anything. We'll have some house n*$*#&@*s do it for us.'"

"I never said that."

"Yes you did, I remember."

It came back to me; I had buried it because it was so hurtful. It was hurtful that Gerrard remembered the time and place it happened. Gerrard used racism to fuel his achievement. He used his anger to reach his goals. He became a doctor, a dentist. He was focused.

Playing Volleyball

We were going up to play volleyball, and we were picking teams. Gerry didn't get picked. I was joking around and said, "Nobody picked you because you're a brother." (It's actually because he sucks at playing volleyball). We were talking after everyone left; he told me I hurt his feelings. He said, "Goldie I know you're not racist, but when you said they didn't pick me because I was a brother, someone might be racist and it brought attention to the fact that I was different. You were singling me out and even though you didn't mean it as a hurtful thing, it hurt."

Racism — a Scar on our Souls

The KKK — in your wildest imagination how could it be that a bunch of people could or would get together and decide everyone who's not like them is bad — and have tens of thousands follow them? How can it happen? How shortsighted. How incredibly un-intelligent. Yet, you see, generation after generation carrying this prejudice. Why is that? Is there any part of this that is good, healthy, better for a person — better for society? How could someone influence others to join their organization, to kill another human being because somebody is a different color? How could someone persecute or hate a person like Gerrard, just because he's a different race? Or me, because my last name's Goldberg?

We Can Change the World

I saw a book about the KKK. In it was a picture of a man with his shotgun, his two boys and his daughter. The kids are holding up the head of a black person, smiling. There also was a picture of people sitting around a man hanged, joking, laughing, and feeling good. What a scar on all of us!

When is killing somebody a viable excuse for not getting along? The answer is obvious — never. Many say they had a bad childhood, a bad upbringing. They make excuses for their behavior, who they are, their shortcomings, what they haven't done, why they're not successful. That's a cop-out, a fragile excuse for not doing what you know you *should* be doing!

We see the rich in the Porsche, living in million dollar homes. All that stuff doesn't make them successful! They're not better than us. We're all just human beings. Take responsibility for who you are. Be kind to others. Treat them as you would have them treat yourself. We all know the difference between right and wrong. We all have shortcomings. We're all racists. Choose to actually be that person you want other people to think that you are. You can change. Choose the good. We can change the world. Change yourself. Change now.

We're all doing our best. But, can't we do better??????????? !!!! duh!!!!!

I Can Do Better

I like to think that I have never used the *n* word. It is such a terrible word, historical hate and racism. It is not okay for anyone to use that word. It is racism. It's a word that defines racism. It implies slave, master, you are not equal, you are a lesser race. What can we do? If you want the world to be a better place, start with yourself. No, not you, me!

26

The Real Me

What's your spin?

What is the mask? The mask is a pretense we hide ourselves behind. Like a shield we hold in front of ourselves. It hides you. It hides me. It's our *front*. A mask is something we want other people to perceive as being the real me, the real you. It's a pretend thing. We present ourselves as a person we want other people to like, love, respect, to care about, follow, appreciate, admire and look up to. But, it's not who we really are. Or, is it? Is that pretend person our idea of who we should be, but don't quite know how to be? Or don't quite have the courage to be? So, we pretend? Think about it.

The Spin

You've probably heard of "the spin"? That picture politicians and others put on happenings and events to make us believe that what they are doing or have done is good or right. Our mask is the spin *we* put out to compel you to believe we are good and right, or maybe competent, confident and successful. Or, if you are a kid, with it and cool, knowing all the latest songs and lingo.

You're Wonderful!

"I hit 20 home runs in Little League when I was 12.", and Paul says, "Um, interesting, I hit 28 and missed two games because of injury. Of course, it was snowing the whole season." We know it was a lie. Paul knows it was a lie, but we laugh, saying, "That's great!"

We know Paul was telling the story to impress us with abilities he *wishes* he had so that we would admire him. We all want that. We want too, perhaps need to like ourselves, see ourselves as good, liked and admired. We want to be appreciated.

The Mask Hides Me From Me

The mask not only hides me from you, but it hides me from myself! Who has the courage to lower the mask to actually understand who he truly is? It's painful, maybe, impossible. We know deep down in our hearts that we are not really that person we pretend to be. And, yet, on a day-to-day, practical basis, it *is* who we *believe* ourselves to be. We believe and we might even, in a way, be a part of our mask. More than anything, we hope you believe my mask is truly who I am. Do you?

Behind the Mask

There are times in our lives when a powerful incident occurs. It might be a death, a birth, a marriage, a sickness, a fight or a breakup. This touching occurrence strikes our emotions which draw the curtain aside. It is there, in our souls and our hearts, that we see a fragment of our true selves. Maybe for a minute, maybe a day, maybe for the rest of our lives!

We might see a terrible mistake we have made, telling a lie or story over and over until it seems like part of us. Or, something we have done that hurt others or our own lives. Others believe us, but *we* know the truth. We always know the truth.

Or, we see our tender self, so tender that only tears can express how sweet and kind and loving we truly are. So gentle that we don't want to show that part to anyone else. They might think we are too meek or too kind.

Don't Look Behind Mine!

The truth is hard to accept. It is hard to believe that we can be that mean or that deceitful, that cruel or that uncaring. It is hard to believe we can weep and feel so tender. When we get that quick glimpse into our true selves, we are torn with hurt. We don't want to see it, we don't want to believe it and we don't want to admit it.

We solve the agony of it all by the clever design of the mask. And we have made this strange agreement: you pretend I don't have a mask and I'll pretend you don't have a mask. Don't look behind mine and I won't look behind yours! To ourselves, we say, "Let's not go there."

The Secret Closet

Behind the mask, veiled in dark, hidden places, we peer to see, to find what's hidden in the closet. In the closet are traits, wrongs, weaknesses that are such failings that we are afraid to take them out of that closet. We lock them in. Even when or if we open that closet, we only allow ourselves to see **portions** of how disappointing we are: times when we have been mean and thoughtless, the mistakes we have made, the hurts we have caused. We don't want to see or know our deep failings, as a parent, son or daughter, sister or brother. We don't dare look. We shudder.

Open the closet Door

So, the question is: do we want to open that closet and look in? And see what is in there? *For me, the answer is Yes!* Why? After we come to terms with the lies, the mistakes and wrong we have done, can we look in the mirror? We don't have a choice. We **must** look in the mirror. We must see who we really are. Why? What good does that do?

That Wrinkled, Throw-Away Part

We will be able to discern the good from the bad, the lies from the truth. We can drag that stuff out, hold it up to the Light and allow it to be transformed. We can change. We have to embrace all of ourselves to heal that part in the closet, to claim the wrinkled, throw-away, soiled part of ourselves on that closet floor. That might be the best part! That part we've thrown away, or tried to hide.

A Quick Peek

We hope to be forgiven by Him who loves us. The harder part is to forgive ourselves. Can we forgive ourselves? Can I love myself after I see the true me? Can we share who we really are with those who love us? Maybe, even see behind the mask? Can we share our innermost feelings, our innermost doubts? Do we dare share who we really are and trust that the other will still care, love, stay with us?

Choose to Forgive.

When you bring any part of yourself out of the closet or even get a glimpse of something bad or wrong you think you have done, there is one thing you must do to heal yourself and anyone else connected and that is forgive. You must forgive the person for any hurt or wrong done to you. And forgive yourself for any hurt or wrong you have done to another. You forgive them because in the forgiving, you heal yourself. And, who knows? You may heal the other too?

Choose to forgive them for their faults. Choose to forgive me for my faults.

Since we know we all pretend to be something we are not, why not choose the positive? Why should I tell you what a farce you are? Why should I send my negative thoughts about you out into the world? See the good in people. Choose the positive. Choose to dwell with the sun in your face. Choose to dwell on the good things that you love about somebody. Dredge up a precious memory or thought. Hold that in the center of your mind. You have a choice.

Freely Forgive

Forgive them even if they don't ask for forgiveness — even if you don't "talk it over".

Free to Choose

I'm not implying that we don't see your faults and you don't see mine. We know they are there. I'm not implying that we don't see our own faults. But, at every moment in every instance, we have a choice to dwell on the good. Even though we all fall short, we all do our best. The mistakes are there; we hold them both, the good and the bad. Guess what? We have a choice to throw away the bad and look at the half full, beautiful, good. We have a choice. It's just that simple.

Try this, put something about your self or the other that you don't like in one hand; put the good and beautiful in the other hand. And then, throw the bad thing away and tell it, "You are gone. Don't come back."

Or, write the bad things on a piece of paper, then, burn it in the fire.

Think Positive

We don't want to wallow in the negative about ourselves or the other. We want to recognize these faults, bring them to the Light, then, discard them. You/he/she/I can't be all bad, can't be perfectly bad, perfectly wrong. Begin to think on the good, the positive — the times you've helped someone, the times you did well, the times someone really liked or appreciated you. Dwell on the truths you've told. Center on the good things you've done. Dwell on the hugs. Recall the kisses. Remember, in every situation, you have a choice. Choose to remember the wonderful things, the great times, the loving moments. Choose to be positive.

Choose the Good.

Choose to see the beautiful things in that friend, parent, daughter, son, mate even though we realize the truth, that the underside is there. Choose the good. It's just that simple. You have a choice. Choose to see the beauty in people. Choose to see the good.

Why the Mask?

The mask exists because of love. Isn't that interesting? That we cover ourselves up and pretend to be what we think might be better because we want you to love us and we want to love you. We create our masks to make ourselves lovable, to make you lovable. See that the reason they told the lie, the reason they portrayed themselves to be somebody they weren't was because they wanted you to like them, wanted you to love them, wanted to impress you. You have a choice. Be happy, see the good in things, see the good in people. Give love.

27

Reading the Book to Dad

Best Day Ever

He looks great. As we walk in, he is flirting hard with a very pretty nurse, something about a bath. He smiles from ear to ear when he sees us. We have the same looks on our faces. The nurse keeps talking even though we show up. She is telling Dad that in order to stay in a relationship, you have to think about the man's good qualities and ignore the bad ones. Richard and I look at each other, we're smiling.

Reading the Book to Dad

"Dad I want to read you the Book, the part about our telephone conversation. It's our true-life experience. It captures the heart of the Book, its true essence. It is the reason for writing it."

So, here we go. I am reading it to him; he is listening. As I am reading, he says, "Your retention is amazing." He keeps interrupting. I read, "When I come to the part about the phone call, when I was trying to call Matt, I picked up the phone and there you were, normally, I would never have answered it because it would have said *Out of the Area,* and there you were."

"I knew you wouldn't have answered if you knew it was me. God was funneling me in there to straighten you out!" Richard and I look at each other. We are blown away. Now he is getting spiritual on us.

I try to continue and he interrupts, "That's not right, that's not who I am, that's not right; I never shaved your head, I cut your hair, you needed a haircut."

"You didn't shave my head with a straight edged razor. You told the barber to, 'Take off all of them curls. Don't make any of it longer than a quarter of an inch.' I think that's called a **butch.** Dad, I am not going to read the book to you unless you listen."

"You make me sound terrible. I was a good father. I am not a racist. I don't want you to portray me as a racist. I was just flirting with that Mexican girl. She was hot."

Dad says, "That's not right." I said 'proud' at least 40 more times than that. I don't like that part about me being so material. I didn't just buy you things."

"Dad, can you just quiet down and listen."

"I want you to hear me, I want to put in my two cents. You can write whatever you want — it is your experience. S**t! That is not who I am. Yeah, I wanted to take care of you boys; if you wanted a horse, I bought you a horse. If Richard wanted a motorcycle, I bought him a motorcycle. I wanted you to have a better life. But, I wasn't just a material dad; I was a good father."

Dad, Do You Trust Me?

"Dad do you trust me?" We all laugh. "Dad, this is important to me. It is from my heart. It is our life together. I want you to listen to it. If you listen to it, you won't have to keep correcting me, telling me how sensitive you are and what a great father you are. That is what *I* am trying to tell you. Can you just listen?"

"Yeah, but — "

"Dad, when I am done, I promise you can talk as long as you want. But do me a favor; don't build your case until you hear the whole story."

Let 'Er Rip, Son

Throughout my Dad's ranting and raving, Richard and I keep looking at each other and laughing. We are excited. We can't wait for him to stop talking and listen. Dad listens, I mean, he really listened. He nodded his head. He was smiling. We were laughing. I keep crying as I am reading; I can't get through it. I am blown away.

"Rich, I need more tissue. Richard, will you just read this for me. I am really struggling here?"

"No, you are doing a great job, you need to read it. I'll get you some more tissue."

Dad says, "It's okay to cry. It's good for you. Let 'er rip, Son, let it all out."

I got through it all. It was incredible. It was so healing. I was crying.

My Dad said, "Come here. I need to hug you."

I was sobbing, bubbles and all. I was hugging him. He was hugging me. Richard was holding our hands.

Dad said, "I am crying on the inside. I can't believe this. This is the best s**t I have ever heard. We are going to be f*#$%%g rich!" We all laugh.

"It's amazing. I am glad you finally figured it out. I wasn't just a material father. I gave you what you needed."

My Best Day Ever

"How do you feel, Dad, how are you feeling right now? I have never felt closer to you." Dad looks at me, with tears in his eyes.

> ***"Son, this is my Best Day Ever.***
> ***If they cut my heart out today,***
> ***it would still be my***
> ***Best Day Ever."***

It's a Miracle

We hug, kiss and share love with each other. It is beautiful. Richard gets a phone call and goes outside. The nurse comes in. I follow Richard outside onto the deck. He hangs up and we look at each other.

Richard says, "It's a miracle."

Right then, a beautiful butterfly lands on the tree directly in front of us.

Richard says, "God, it is so beautiful."

"The butterfly or what happened to us with Dad?"

"Dad, but the butterfly, too."

We are seeing our Father as this amazing loving, intelligent, humorous man.

I Can't Stop Smiling

"Hey, that butterfly left something on the tree. Look at the way it flies — through the middle of the tree and never hits anything — an egg, a caterpillar, a chrysalis, a butterfly." I reach out and pick the branch. It seems like our thoughts are confirmed: nature has answered our question for us; a big fat slug can take a little time, dwell on the positive, see the good and wake up transformed into a beautiful butterfly.

Alone, in the Dark

In less than a week, my relationship with my Dad was transformed. It was the one thing in my life, the one thing that hurt the most, that I couldn't fix. I carried all that baggage, all that hurt; now, I keep remembering the wonderful things he did. It was what I prayed for, alone, in the dark, the one thing that could make me whole, with a complete Father and Son connection. I didn't smile when I thought about my Father, I left hurt. Now, I can't stop smiling.

I am healed. My Father is healed.

Tears of Joy

On the way home, Richard is driving; Moe is lying on my lap. I am smiling. *Here Comes the Sun — it's alright now* welcomes us as we make our way over the Grapevine. I keep smiling, you know, a perfect smile. Rich keeps looking over at me and says, "What?" "I was just thinking about Dad. I never smiled when I thought about Dad. Now, when I think of him, I can't stop smiling." Rich reaches over and holds my hand. We both have tears of joy streaming down our faces. It's perfect. It's peaceful.

"I don't know how it happened, Rich. I have never felt more in touch with my Father. Our relationship has been transformed."

28

Who Do I Choose to be Today?

It's just that simple

In less than a week, my relationship with my dad was transformed. We realized how powerful this was and struggled to figure it out. Hour after hour pacing, what happened? How can this happen? Is it really just that simple? This is blowing us away. What allowed us to see the positive in our dad?

It's Just That Simple

Wow! Can it be that simple? Stop. Close your eyes. Think about how powerful this is!!!!!!!!!! Was I crazy then? Or, am I crazy now?

We do have a choice!!!!!! Are you listening? Close your eyes; think about it — do you want to be a big fat caterpillar or a beautiful butterfly? Yeah, but I can't change overnight.

I Had a Choice

All I had to do was to see the good, see the positive, dwell on the good, dwell on the positive. I saw his passion. I dwelt on his passion. It's so easy if you do it. It's so easy if I do it. It's so easy to choose the good. The positive always outweighs the negative. I am a free individual. I can choose whatever I want as the focus or point of view to hold. I have a choice. I chose to see the bad things about my Father. I chose to dwell on the bad. I chose to share the bad with my family and friends. "My Dad's a real prick, but I love him." I have been saying that for 25 years. I had choice. I have a choice.

Now, I choose to see love, I choose to see caring. I choose to see the good in my Father. It was always there; I just didn't choose to see it.

My Best Day Ever!

It's my best day ever. No. Really, I mean it. I am living it. I am healed. My Father is healed. It's so f*&&Ing simple. Is it really just this easy? Do I really have a choice to be happy in any situation?

No matter how hurtful? No matter how important? No matter how long I have been carrying it around? No matter how long I have been building my case? No matter how long I haven't heard him? No matter how long I have been formulating my answer? Always dwelling on the bad sh*t? YES! It is just that simple.

A Caterpillar or a Butterfly

Who or what determines who we become? Is it our parents, our upbringing, the environment in which we are raised? Is our destiny already written? Do we have a choice? Do I have the ability to change? Could I possibly change overnight? Grow? Could I grow from a caterpillar into a butterfly? From a slug, crawling along on a branch? To become a beautiful butterfly? Experience a metamorphosis just because it's what I choose to do? Is my mind/body/soul/heart able to take a little time out? Step back and look at who I am and become the person I would have my child be with nothing more than mental toughness?

It Has to Start With Me

To save the world, it has to start with me. If we choose to become the person we are capable of being today, that is the most powerful thing you or I can do to contribute to the world — a role model for the world.

How to be the person we are capable of being? We know the difference between right and wrong. We always know the difference.

Do I, You, We have the heart, the courage to attack the most challenging incident we will ever face? Today is the first day of the rest of our lives. So, here we go. Do the right thing every time. Forty-eight hours out of your life. What have you got to lose? When you get cut off, smile and wave instead of giving them the finger. Throw out the peace sign. Never let an asshole ruin your day.

One Week to Live

We have one week to live, seven days to right our wrongs, move on without regrets. Get out a pen and paper and write all the things we need to set right before we die. There are many things we've been holding onto, avoiding, putting off, such hard things to deal with, blaming someone else for our own lies and weaknesses. If it's on the list, fix it.

Humble From Your Heart

Reach out and humble yourself. Does that sound offensive? No, it is patient and kind. It shows love. Admit we're human and we've made many mistakes. "Please forgive me. I am truly sorry. I want to take your pain away; I want to take my pain away. I beg you to forgive me. Will you? Will you forgive me?" Make it real. Humble from your heart.

My Mom started to talk to me about her mother dying. As she did, she began crying. I asked her, "Mom, what are you feeling?" "Adam, I'm not sure she knew how much I loved her. I was in such a hurry about living my own life. I wish I had told her." Ouch! Let everyone you love know how you feel about them. Don't leave anything unfinished

The List

Everybody's list will be different. When you make your list, no qualifying. Everything you think of, write down: world peace, feed the hungry, financial freedom, no more racism. Yeah, they're on my list, too. Your list has to start with you. No, not you, *me.* The things you need to change in your lives are personal. The things I need to change in my life are personal. Let's do it together.

It's Time to be Real

My list is huge. Some of it is pretty scary stuff. Your commitment is one hundred and sixty-eight hours (assumptive close) so let's make a top ten list. Keep the rest. Don't you dare leave that one out! It's time to be real.

Yesterday, Tomorrow, Today

Yesterday is gone, but we learned from it. Tomorrow is uncertain but we can plan for it. Today is the one time that is truly real. How many times have you **tried** to do it? If you just try, you will fail. For the next seven days and nights, no excuses, no cheating. Mental toughness. This will change your life and everyone you touch will be better because of it.

Don't Try. Do It

Our goal is to fix the first one. Start with the one that means the most to your personal life. Now that that's done, we can move on to the next one. It's okay to share it with friends and family. Most will support and encourage you. They might be surprised and want to join you in your expedition. Don't tell them you're going to **try**. Tell them you are going to **do** it. If there's no one you want to share it with, that's okay.

We Will Succeed

We will succeed. Leave no doubt in our minds. I am truly the only one that can change me. You are the only one that can change you. It's a commitment that only requires **you** and **me**.

Pledge

I will be loving, positive, kind, honest, healthy, passionate, humble, listening. I will take the right path. I will stop blaming my upbringing, my mother, my father, my sister, my brother for who I am. I will stop blaming my wife or husband for my failures. **I take all responsibility for who I am**. I will succeed.

One week out of your life is what we are talking about. How can it possibly hurt you? To have every day be **your** Best Day Ever? To fix all that stuff we've been carrying around. If it's not your fault, fix it anyway. Forgive yourself. Forgive them. They will be healed with you.

Adam's List

Publish this book
Make friends with Dad
Save everyone
Take over the world, one heart at a time
Make millions
Spend millions
Be a better husband, son, friend, father

A Hint of a Smile

At 11:30 Thanksgiving Day, I thought, "I've got to call my Father for Thanksgiving." Adriana answered and said, "He's napping. I've got to wake him. He told me, 'If Adam calls, be sure to wake me.'" I had a hint of a smile on my face.

Dad was on the line.

My Father poured his heart out to me. He told me stories that he told me when I was a kid. He was sharing. He was reaching out. He was growing. And I loved it.

At the end of the conversation, Dad said, "We had a really nice talk, didn't we, Son? It was great talking to you. I'll call you tomorrow."

Don't Give Up

Don't give up. Mental toughness. We all have bad days. We could have got right back in the familiar rut. We're no longer comfortable there. Mental toughness.

Feels good to be happy. Feels good to love your Father and know that he loves you, too. Did I mention that he really is proud of me? Did I mention that we really do love each other?

How's your day?

I hope you know how to answer that question.

Thanks for reading My Book. Thanks for letting me share BEST DAY EVER with you. I love knowing you are choosing the good, dwelling on the positive, quickly forgiving with me.

Wishing you blessings galore.

D. Adam Goldberg

CPSIA information can be obtained at www.ICGtesting.com
Printed in the USA
BVOW032341251112

306379BV00005B/14/P